Perfect Pitch
in the Key of
Autism

Perfect Pitch
in the Key of
Autism

A Guide for Educators, Parents, and the Musically Gifted

Henny Kupferstein
and
Susan Rancer

PERFECT PITCH IN THE KEY OF AUTISM
A Guide for Educators, Parents, and the Musically Gifted

Copyright © 2016 Henny Kupferstein & Susan Rancer.

All rights reserved. No part of this book may be used or reproduced by any means, graphic, electronic, or mechanical, including photocopying, recording, taping or by any information storage retrieval system without the written permission of the author except in the case of brief quotations embodied in critical articles and reviews.

Cover Artwork by: Loretta G. Breuning

iUniverse books may be ordered through booksellers or by contacting:

iUniverse
1663 Liberty Drive
Bloomington, IN 47403
www.iuniverse.com
1-800-Authors (1-800-288-4677)

Because of the dynamic nature of the Internet, any web addresses or links contained in this book may have changed since publication and may no longer be valid. The views expressed in this work are solely those of the author and do not necessarily reflect the views of the publisher, and the publisher hereby disclaims any responsibility for them.

ISBN: 978-1-5320-0142-0 (sc)
ISBN: 978-1-5320-0141-3 (e)

Library of Congress Control Number: 2016910397

Print information available on the last page.

iUniverse rev. date: 07/20/2016

Contents

Introduction xi
Chapter One: Very Musical, Talented—and Quirky 1
   i. Auditory Memory 5
   ii. Screening for Absolute Pitch 5
   iii. Screening for Relative Pitch 8
   iv. Practical Application 10
   v. Case Studies: Students with Absolute and Relative Pitch 13
   vi. Inquiries 14
Chapter Two: Absolute Pitch—Why It Matters 19
   i. Prodigies and Savants 20
   ii. Absolute Pitch is Not a Curse 23
   iii. Visual Processing Challenges 25
   iv. Reading Comprehension and Eye Movement 29
Chapter Three: Right Brain/Left Brain Learning Traits 35
   i. LBAP/RBAP: Henny's Variations Theory 36
   ii. RBAP vs. LBAP Assessment 37
   iii. Success Stories 46
Chapter Four: Why Start With Piano? 48
   i. First Steps 50
   ii. Case Studies: Physical Challenges 52

    iii. Free Time 53
    iv. Case Studies: Self-Esteem and Cognition 55
    v. Sight-Reading and Piano Notation...................................56
    vi. Important Do's and Don'ts..59
    vii. Autistic Students..63
    viii. Learning Styles..66
    ix. Auditory Learners 67
    x. Important Notes...73
    xi. Feedback and Frequently Asked Questions....................75

Chapter Five: Music Therapy 83
    i. Examples of Standard Music Therapy Goals 86
    ii. Examples of Client-Specific Goals 87
    iii. How to Incorporate the Goals of Music Therapy 89
    iv. Methodology 92
    v. Special Education 93
    vi. Anecdotes 94
    vii. Therapists Without Absolute Pitch 95
    viii. Free-Time Activities 97
    ix. Establishing Your Private Practice 101
    x. Marketing your Private Practice.....................................103

Chapter Six: Our Fail-Proof Method 108
    i. Piano Pedagogy: Structuring the Lesson......................108
    ii. Solfege and Intervals Training 116
    iii. Practice 120
    iv. Teaching Strategies 122
    v. Teaching Guitar...129

Chapter Seven: Accommodating The Individual Gift 133
    i. Assessing for Absolute Pitch...135
    ii. Non-Verbal Testing Method 136
    iii. Your Language 139
    iv. Scales and Rote Learning 141
    v. Case Study: Auditory Learner 143
    vi. Sensory Issues..144
    vii. Misunderstood Stimming 150

viii. Synesthesia 153
ix. Hyperlexia, Dyscalculia, Prosopagnosia, and
    Photographic Memory 161

Chapter Eight: How Do Savants Do It? 164
  i. Splinter Skills 165
  ii. Alpha Waves and Right-Brain Perceptual Processing 167

Chapter Nine: Autism and Sensory Intergration 171
  i. Absolute Pitchers' Stimming 172
  ii. Musicality 175
  iii. Learning as a Spectrum 176
  iv. Early Intervention 177
  v. Coda: In the Key of Henny 178

About the Authors

Henny Kupferstein, M.A. is a doctoral student of psychology with a specialization in autism research. She is also a musical savant with absolute pitch and synesthesia. Henny gives web-based piano lessons to non-verbal and autistic students around the world. She is a parent of autistic children and is an autistic scholar, composer, and researcher. Henny is a contributing author, appearing in six chapters in the book "Been There, Done That, Try This!", edited by Tony Attwood, Craig R. Evans and Anita Lesko. Henny can be reached via www.HennyK.com

Susan Rancer, RMT is a Registered Music Therapist since 1975. She has absolute pitch and was a child prodigy, and performed on the piano from a young age. She maintains a private practice in the San Francisco Bay Area where she does music therapy with special needs clients. She is the Author of Teaching Music to the Special Needs Client: A Music Therapist's Approach (ch. 25) in the book "Islands of Genius" by Dr. Darold Treffert, who is the world's expert on savants. In 2005, Susan published a short booklet titled "Perfect Pitch Relative Pitch", a guide for identifying and testing for the phenomena. Susan can be reached via www.SusanRancer.com

Introduction

Susan and Henny only work with students who have special needs and who could not otherwise benefit from lessons with a piano teacher in their local community. "We start all of our beginning clients *from scratch* with a no-fail method. By showing them their own success from the start, they don't give up". They focus on the process of teaching them, where the standard music teacher focuses on the product, or performance at the upcoming recital. The Rancer Method is their evidence-based piano pedagogy designed to access open channels of learning with the expectation that the absolute pitch student requires a different mode or presentation due to processing differences. The method organizes an appropriate sequence of material that is freely available at the local music store.

This book answers the three questions: Why Piano? Why a music therapist? Why do we care about absolute pitch? The original focus of our research was to explain the seeming connection between absolute pitch and learning disabilities. What we discovered was that there are no learning disabilities. There are learning *differences* and brilliant tactics that enable coping with each of those differences, tools that lead to success in academics and all areas of functioning. In addition, you will find a Q&A section, bulleted lists of giftedness tendencies, and case studies.

What is perfect pitch? Also known as "Absolute Pitch" ("AP" in the literature) is defined as the ability to identify the pitch of a musical tone by name without an external reference pitch. Some research suggests that only 1 in 10,000 individuals have this ability[1]. Absolute pitch is better understood as a spectrum of abilities[2], not all of which conform to this highest standard of skill. In its fundamental form, AP is a photographic memory for sound.

The motivation their students have for making great-sounding music is what keeps them pushing through incredible barriers to get to where they are making music independently. Anyone who knows about sensory issues and gross, fine, and motor planning challenges can appreciate the joy they show in the videos of their playing. Many teachers struggle to figure out how to teach their students theory and technique. We say, let them play it first and then analyze the theory of whatever they just played. That is the fun part for the absolute pitcher, just like professional chefs enjoy picking apart a dish only after they've tasted it. Such a student won't learn if playing scales and rote learning is pushed onto him, no matter how motivated he is. Forcing someone to learn in a manner that is not conducive to their learning style is like painting the potholes bright yellow so the blind student can cross the street better.

Oliver started taking piano lessons with Henny when he was 12. Autistic and non-speaking, he types to communicate. He also experienced severe motor planning issues and needed hands-on support by an attending adult. As a distance (Skype) student, Henny relied on Oliver's mother to squeeze his hands in a specific way to allow him to independently move his fingers. To the untrained observer, it would appear as if his mother was doing all the playing, by pressing close to his fingers. In a matter of weeks he transitioned into playing independently with all ten fingers. One year later Oliver only needed the occasional elbow support for one or both arms.

Oliver's mother posted some videos on their blog, including this comment: "There is so much to tell you, really. How I found

---

[1] Bossomaier, T., & Snyder, A. (2004). Absolute pitch accessible to everyone by turning off part of the brain?. *Organised Sound,* 9(02), 181-189.

[2] Bachem, A. (1937). Various types of absolute pitch. *Journal of the Acoustical Society of America.*

this awesome, incredible teacher. How she recognizes his strengths and teaches to them. How she effortlessly assumes his competency even when I'm still not sure! How she totally gets how he processes information. How I always leave a lesson thinking: Well, this next step is going to be hard! And then how it totally isn't even a fraction as hard as I imagined! Just thinking about it makes me want to explode with happiness".

One of the goals that Susan and Henny work on throughout the sessions is to prove to the family and teachers how intelligent the students are. For example, Henny says, "Last week, I asked my 4-year-old student to pull down the lid on the piano (covering the keys). I instructed him to turn the page to a new song he's never seen before, and pretend-play on the piano lid while singing the alphabet. For parents seeing their kid sight-sing by pulling notes out of his head is like watching a flower bloom right in front of their eyes." When those parents are musically trained, they usually just start crying. In this student's case, there was a therapist present who had a very low opinion of this poor little kid until she saw him nailing this new piece.

If you are a professional music teacher or music therapist, you'll know the musical terms you will encounter in this book. However, other readers may need a bit of explanation for commonly used terms in musical lingo. Our definitions which may appear redundant at times are intentional with hope that a parent with a special-needs child can understand how our method differs from traditional teaching, and thus suddenly see an opportunity to enrich their child's life through music. We hope you will benefit from the book's unique insights, methods, and approach, enabling you to pass along what you have learned to your own musicianship, your students, and your loved ones.

Henny recently consulted with a piano/voice teacher for her upcoming lesson with a 13-year-old autistic student. He's been resisting learning sight-singing and note-reading. The teacher said, "What if I let him sing on la-la-la, or numbers, or pronounce the letter names" and Henny responded, "what if you present to him a song in C, and let him sing the lyrics, attaching the pitch he already hears in his head?"

Later in the day, Henny observed the lesson, and the student did exceptionally well. He learned five intervals (distances between two notes such as "a second" or "a third") and identified them all by interval name rather than pitches (e.g. "C" or "D") with his back to the piano. This is a standard approach to ear training for sight-singing which is singing something for the first time from written music. Next, he learned one new song from scratch, sight-singing without knowing that he was doing precisely that. At the last measure, there was a short divisi (two-part duo), and he held his own while the teacher (1) accompanied on piano, and (2) sang the mezzo part. The teacher was quite blown away by all the talent that was brought out by simply working to his strengths. Instead of his lessons being a waste of time and "musical babysitting" (Henny's term), this kid began the beautiful journey towards exceptional musicianship.

In contrast, college music majors are pressured to learn rapidly and are expected to excel in sight-singing by singing in solfege (e.g. "do, re, mi" etc.). Henny's friend Nicole DiPaolo (pianist/composer/teacher in Indiana) says she "developed good relative pitch just as a consequence of general music training." How true, since absolute pitchers come in two breeds: those who learned solfege before pitch, and those who learned pitch before solfege. The latter find themselves in a deep struggle in musical challenges. Henny was really fortunate to have learned solfege before she even knew that the keys on the piano had letter names. As a result, she thinks in fixed solfege. Sitting in her car, she can listen to the radio, hear an F#, and yelp out "fi!" at other drivers. Jason Madore, a vocalist in Minneapolis, MN has expressed his frustration to Henny: *"Oh God, I HATE doing solfege. I'm about as skilled at it as I am at massaging an electric eel".*

Absolute pitch is the powerhouse for A., a 7-year-old student with Cerebral Palsy presenting with stiffness throughout her whole body. Her fingers have been gaining accuracy on the piano because she has been using her ear as a guide to know where to adjust her finger placement across the keyboard. Making perfect-sounding music motivates her to keep pushing through the extensive efforts in rewiring her brain each day in her practice.

An ear-based auditory learner has a gift. If we see that this student has difficulty with processing, we have to wake up his visual skills from the beginning so that he can eventually catch up to his exceptional ear, connecting the two and thereby achieving well-rounded mastery. The ear stays intact, and grows as we move along in the process. When the students are ready, the integration between the eyes and ears have been bridged, so they can capitalize on their now more powerful gift.

The Rancer Method was created and implemented by Susan Rancer, a music therapist in the Bay Area of California. Since 1975, Susan has seen clients in her private practice with diagnoses that vary from autism to ADHD to Down syndrome. She immediately noticed a trend in her students: The majority displayed signs of absolute pitch. People asked, "How can you tell?" The answer: Because she has it too! When Henny graduated with a four-year degree in music, she could play everything she heard but could not read any notes. Susan then started Henny on the method from the bottom up, and Henny was note-reading at college level within six weeks. This book provides a rich array of insights on how to apply the method. If you are a parent of a special-needs child, we hope you will be inspired to make music be a vibrant part of your child's life.

By allowing other absolute pitchers to observe her practice, Susan has connected with many people who have confirmed that they too can see the signs of an absolute pitcher. Once Susan began to make note of these subtle signs, more and more people began to identify with these characteristic traits. Thus they find their own place in the AP spectrum, where no two absolute pitchers are alike. Now with our expanded list of traits, our method is easily learned, scientifically proven, and critical for educators to employ so as to best serve their students.

Every absolute pitcher experiences music in a similar way. They also experience life in a similar way. Not all, but many, struggle tremendously with reading comprehension and math in similar ways. Some also fail miserably when attempting to sight-read sheet music. We wondered why. If many of us have the same issues, then is it appropriate for a music teacher to inflict sight-reading on us using the traditional methods if they're clearly not working? We will answer that question too. More important, if we develop sight-reading ability, will our skills be accepted as correct by the standards of the classical tradition if we were taught them differently? We believe it will.

Traditional sight-reading is focused on the product with the performance being the end result. We are focused on the process. This defining difference is inherent in the training for music therapists versus that for music educators. This is because it's within the process itself that magic happens, as the brain rewires itself not only for sight-reading but also for every other area of functioning. Thus, when done correctly, sight-reading exercises also strengthen reading comprehension and mathematics.

In Susan's practice, students often have to be waitlisted. One human being can see only about fifty clients a week before using up every waking hour. Desperate parents who contact Susan to be placed on the waiting list, all have a similar story. Some call after their child was recently diagnosed with a special need, and they've been told about the benefits of music therapy, though they know little about it. Others call because their child, sans diagnosis, has failed with every music teacher she ever went to, yet the child seems very gifted. Still others call because they have a child who seems very musical. In contrast, Henny carefully selects her caseload, preferring nonverbal students from underserved areas to teach them via Skype.

This is the beginning of the process. When they walk through the door, the assessment process for testing for absolute pitch begins immediately. The common trend among all the above-described people is that they all have absolute pitch but don't know it. Susan quips, "They all have absolute pitch until proven otherwise". Those circumstances are typical in the life of an absolute pitcher. They include low self-esteem, explosive situations with music educators, and an extreme need for sound in one's life. That paradox is astounding. When the session begins, we learn that all of these people also struggle in other areas in life, some of them academic areas such as reading comprehension, mathematics, and language. On the other hand, some of them excel at these skills, which baffled both Henny and Susan.

Susan identified the problem when she realized that teachers don't know how to work with such kids, send them away due to frustration, and then blame the children for their own failures. Henny is adamant about providing clues from inside her brain to help complete the picture.

Susan and Henny were brought together by their mutual giftedness. When people with absolute pitch (AP) realize that they learn very differently, their journey begins as a very lonely one. Susan always thought she was weird because she was Jewish and from Amarillo, Texas. Henny always thought she was weird because that's what people told her all her life. So many people with absolute pitch (AP) react the same way as we did. Unless a person actively analyzes herself and reads through the research and does lots of Google searching, she will feel like she is nuts and is the only one on the planet who thinks like she does. Often, these people are merely marching to the tune of a different drummer, one way out in left field.

At thirty-two, Henny was in the classroom studying Intro to Music Theory for the first time. As the teacher went up and down the rows, she asked each student to sight-sing about four measures using the solfege syllables ("do-re-mi") taught that day. After each student sang, the teacher would give the next one the starting pitch (the sound of "do") on the piano. When it was Henny's turn, she just launched right into singing without that prompt. Though the key was the same as the previous student's snippet, this particular melody started from the higher "do" and moved down in a descending pattern. Beginner sight-singers should not be able to nail that without a reference point, but most absolute pitchers don't realize that—they think that everyone thinks like they do.

When the teacher asked, "Henny, do you know if you have absolute pitch?" Henny said, "Um, I don't know." In reality, she didn't know what it meant and had to google the term. When she discovered the definition, she was floored. Suddenly, everything about her personality and what makes her tick started to make sense. Taking it to the next level, Henny googled "autism and perfect pitch," and Susan Rancer's chapter in Dr. Treffert's book, *Islands of Genius,* showed up. After reading it, her heart thumping, Henny cried with the realization that there were others just like her, and her situation now had a name! Her first phone call to Susan that day lasted almost four hours.

Susan professes that the first time she spoke with Henny was like coming full circle. For her entire life she'd felt there was more to this puzzle; that something greater was really happening than she could put her finger on. Speaking with Henny unlocked the doors to the mystery and brought it into real terms. On an emotional level, though, speaking to someone who totally "gets it" is very liberating. Slowly, the collective "we" made its way into their conversations; now it was all about "because that's how we think." It all makes sense now, because another human being thinks like that too. When this project first began, the emotional roller coaster multiplied as more and more absolute pitchers came out of the woodwork to prove that it was indeed absolute pitch that united us on a very deep level. To make that statement, and to demonstrate why the rest of the world should care about the information, we needed to turn to the experts.

To Susan, the journey has been lonely for too long. When she was six years old, she attended a back-to-school night and had the opportunity to play a piano for the first time. Her teacher played in the classroom daily, and Susan, having never touched a piano before in her life, followed by playing every song the teacher played, with two hands. Her parents purchased a piano immediately and started lessons for Susan. The teacher, though, played everything for her first, as many teachers do, and Susan played them right back for her. Susan learned to follow the pictures in the book, associating them with the songs played. As a result, when asked, Susan was able to play something when the book was opened to a specific page, yet no one realized that, rather than sight-reading, she was playing back the songs the teacher had played for her.

That teacher later quit teaching children of Susan's age. Susan was then sent to a teacher with a pink baby-grand piano, which she had painted herself, on a matching pink-painted studio floor. This teacher put a sheet of music without pictures on the piano and said, "play", but Susan couldn't. The teacher then asked, "Do you know why?"

Naturally, Susan couldn't figure it out, as she was only six at the time, so, knowing how talented she was, she made it clear to the teacher that she could play better than her. The teacher then proceeded to test Susan for absolute pitch, and she indeed did have it. It took two painful years of attempted learning to read the music, all taught the traditional way. Though Susan did finally learn, it was a grueling experience. Susan remained with that teacher until middle school, and then switched to a teacher who was a graduate of Columbia University and a very skilled educator. This teacher never figured out that Susan had absolute pitch, but it didn't matter since she was teaching Susan visually.

Fifteen years ago, a colleague showed Susan some videos and she immediately identified the absolute pitchers just by observing their behavior. That's when the colleague said, "I think you're onto something." When Susan reached out to her colleague's music therapy professor at his university, the professor told Susan, "You're on an island, and you're all by yourself." He then invited her to begin writing. This was when Susan contacted Dr. Darold Treffert, who asked her to write a chapter for his upcoming book.

Dr. Darold Treffert has devoted his lifelong practice of psychiatry to studying savants. In every waking hour, Dr. Treffert has advocated for these mysterious humans, entering the no-man's land others didn't want to touch. If not for Dr. Treffert's research and fierce advocacy, the rest of the world would have its way, shutting out savants and excluding the inherent genius of many savants from sharing their gift.

Dr. Treffert pioneered the movement of engaging people in the dialogue around savant abilities. The thought-provoking question is: "If they haven't been taught, but can do something splendidly well, then should we say that they are not masters?" It is important to value the end result rather than the process. For the rest of the world, the process is how they will arrive somewhere in life. Without an education they cannot rise through the ranks. For savants, and many other gifted individuals, this process is literally upside down. It is imperative in their process to value the result, regardless of the process. Thanks to Dr. Treffert, the term "Idiot Savant" has been dissolved, and "Savant Syndrome" has become the term properly applied to individuals with savant abilities.

On a psychological level, it is important to assess for and recognize absolute pitch. These individuals who possess it are dramatically different, and should be allowed to feel like they belong with an in-crowd of their same type. Absolute pitchers who gather around in groups are quite the eclectic bunch. The mastery of music and the expressive musicality is often astounding. Even more so, once someone analyzes herself, she then develops a very strong radar, and can spot an absolute pitcher a mile away.

Susan and Henny can now spot an absolute pitcher merely from watching a YouTube clip. The behaviors are there and are similar across the board. For example, Henny noticed that absolute-pitchers move on the off-beat (e.g. clapping hands on beat 2 and 4 instead of 1 and 3, or shifting weight from right to left foot on the off beat rather than moving to the 1st and 3rd beat of the song). Susan noticed that many of her students are able to sight-sing without a reference (e.g. music played on an instrument) on pitch after only several lessons. Both of us noticed that people all over the world who have absolute pitch will always know that they played a wrong note and start from the beginning of the piece to correct themselves. This is so they can hear the whole phrase as it was intended to be heard.

If 1 in 50 now has autism, wouldn't you think that at least 1 in 50 of the population would have absolute pitch? Statistics on the phenomenon claim that absolute pitch occurs in only 1 in 10,000. This is because people still mistakenly believe that absolute pitch is a sign of extreme intelligence, when it is not—it's merely a phenomenon that occurs in a given individual's brain.

In the case of the autistic brain, the neurology responsible for all other areas of functioning also leaks out this gift. There is much speculation about a very high correlation between absolute pitch and autism spectrum disorders, yet in some research, "surprisingly," the statistics are less than 10% in the autism population.[3] In our study, we found a near 100% correlation between autism and absolute pitch when shifting the paradigm to a more inclusive and neurodiversity-friendly, nonverbal testing method.[4]

Why do we see these vast differences? Because through published articles the bar keeps being raised, so that more and more people are excluded. Autistic people have long been excluded from these studies, in many instances because of their language difficulties.

In scientific terms, the defining criterion for absolute pitch is now a rigid "Thou shalt note name." If one cannot walk down the street and say, "This car horn is honking in C#" then by their definition one does not have absolute pitch. The Rancer Method expands that criterion by including the brilliance of autistic individuals, all with absolute pitch.

The struggles of the absolute pitchers are identical. They all have similar stories of being beaten down for what they couldn't do. Many absolute and relative pitchers struggled in school in academic areas, while displaying "genius" in music. This paradox is often misunderstood, and picked on by educators: "Come on, you're so smart, just buckle down." Absolute pitchers with extreme right brains cannot try harder to do better.

Through this book, we aim to change this—and now, and radically. We intend to restore dignity to those who have been beaten down for their differences, and that means developing recognition for their abilities. The Rancer Method recognizes, assesses, and then taps into those abilities and helps bridge the gap between stark abilities and consuming inabilities.

---

[3] Heaton, et al. (2008), Autism and pitch processing splinter skills: A group and subgroup analysis. Autism: *The International Journal of Research and Practice,* 12 (2) 203–219.

[4] Kupferstein, H., Walsh, B (2015) "Non-Verbal Paradigm for Assessing Individuals for Absolute Pitch," *World Futures,* DOI, 10.1080/02604027.2014.989780.

Chapter One

Very Musical, Talented— and Quirky

What does "very musical" mean? We hear these comments all the time:

"I got frustrated when I took piano lessons, so I quit."
"My teacher always told me that I didn't practice enough."
"She couldn't learn to play piano with her other music teacher."
"I don't like to play the piano anymore."

Students with a highly developed sense of pitch have a special talent that many music teachers don't recognize. With the wrong instructor or instruction technique, a sensitive ear may actually become a handicap to learning, particularly when instructors are more eye oriented than ear oriented. The purpose of this guide is to improve the understanding of absolute pitch (also known as "perfect pitch") and its spectrum so that instructors, students, and parents can all realize the full potential of the musical learning environment.

The philosophy of the Rancer Method is based on our research, which was published in 2015. Ninety-seven percent (all except one) of the autistic people we tested demonstrated absolute pitch. With this information, we explored all the additional cognitive processing differences in the autistic brain and added that to the existing research on absolute pitch. What we discovered was that at least 50 percent of the population might potentially *not* be visual learners. Especially with the perfect-pitch autistic clients, all of the auditory learners also had a convergence insufficiency, making reading nearly impossible at first. Susan and Henny teach to the gift rather than exhausting the student.

Students with absolute pitch and autism will likely come to your piano studio already playing by ear. You want to get them creating sound from written material immediately. You *do not* want to burden them with note reading in the first few weeks lest you turn them away. Instead, use the *Keyboard Talent Hunt* books by Schaum Publications (both books 1 and 2 are for the pre-primer level student). These have all-caps letters printed. You run through the book once with the right hand and then again (only the first half of the book) with the left hand. In book 2, more letters represent right and left-hand notes to be played simultaneously. Songs in both C and G position are written with lyrics. These are melodies that your students do not know, which forces them to read; however, the reading is simple (letters) and gets them making quality intelligent music right away.

By the time students finish book 2, they have flawless fingering and rhythmic awareness, as well as counterpoint and chord-playing skills. They don't know that, but they're starting from the top down in learning. This research-based method relies on the neuroscience concept that the autistic brain masters the complex first (and instantly) but struggles to break down tasks into foundational elements. Therefore, teach the complex stuff and watch students fly. First, *My Piano Book "A"* (Stewart, Glasscock & Glover, Belwin-Mills Publishing Corp, 1985) is used only to teach the notes (from pages 7-25). Next, transition into the *Alfred Basic Piano* series. Now, note reading can begin.

You can easily see that this is a formula for success. Three of Susan's clients have gone on to college. One recently came home for Spring Break, and told Susan that he is on the dean's list. Henny's students are all doing phenomenally. Henny consulted with nineteen of Susan's students in the summer of 2013, and more than half were mainstreamed for the following school year when they demonstrated their intelligence to the school district. In this book, the method is presented as page-by-page instructions, so that every teacher can follow it and do well by their students.

Researchers understand the prevalence of absolute pitch, but fail to recognize that many people have some absolute pitch abilities that are difficult to test. Individuals who cannot and might never be able to read music and therefore "name the notes as they are played" are left out of the statistical count. Individuals with intermittent or key-specific versions of absolute pitch skills are also left out. This is unfortunate, as people with lesser versions of the absolute pitch phenomena share many characteristics and learning styles with those at the highest end of the AP spectrum.

A gene-research study that seeks to find the key to absolute pitch in our DNA inheritance is currently underway at the University of California in San Francisco. If a gene or gene combination responsible for this phenomenon is identified, the concept of absolute pitch and its spectrum may be more widely accepted in the teaching realm.

Are there different levels of absolute pitch and relative pitch? Dr. Darold Treffert, an expert on musical savants (nearly all of whom have strong forms of absolute pitch) describes absolute pitch levels as lying along a spectrum.[5] For example, some students can name notes only on the instrument they are learning to play. Others can name notes only within a five-key range. Still others can hear a bell sound or even a vacuum cleaner and correctly name the note. Many people possessing some degree of absolute pitch "have good days and bad days," and can't always name pitches accurately. Regardless of their degree of absolute or absolute-relative pitch, these individuals all share numerous characteristic behaviors and learning patterns. For example, Susan likes to question people with significant music

---

[5] Dr. Darold Treffert has studied Savant Syndrome as a psychiatrist for over 40 years and is recognized nationally as an expert on this extraordinary condition. His work has had wide distribution in a variety of media. He was also a consultant for the movie Rain Man.

education: "do you think of music in intervals or pitch?" If they think of music in pitches, they are absolute pitchers; if they think of music in intervals, they are relative pitchers. Another trait is an absolute pitcher who denies having absolute pitch, either because they have never been identified under a more inclusive definition, or because they mistakenly believe they need to be perfect all the time. Asking them these two questions is an appropriate screening to open the dialogue.

Why is understanding absolute pitch so important? Individuals with any degree of absolute pitch learn differently than those without it. If taught using conventional methods, students in the absolute pitch spectrum may become unmotivated and their talents could be left undeveloped. However, when these students are encouraged appropriately, music talent may blossom in dramatic ways. Flexibility is absolutely essential when teaching those with absolute pitch because these students process information differently. Teachers without absolute pitch sometimes misconstrue behavioral or learning problems in students when they should, in fact be respecting a gift. An innovative teaching strategy is very important when teaching music to those with extraordinary talent.

What is relative pitch? There are many different variations and degrees of pitch-matching ability. The most common of these variations is relative pitch, which is the ability to identify a pitch once a leading tone is provided as a reference point (note: everyone within the absolute pitch spectrum also possesses relative pitch). Although relative pitch often operates on a lower level of intensity than absolute pitch, many innovative teaching strategies for relative pitch should be the same as for those with absolute pitch.

How are those with absolute pitch and relative pitch different from those without it? When a student with absolute or relative pitch reads a simple song or plays a melodious piece of music for the first time, he or she involuntarily processes it in his or her auditory memory. The piece is captured, much like a tape recording. Once this process has occurred, the visual component of the musical piece can be removed and the student can play the same piece of music without any reference to the notes.

In contrast to an absolute pitch learner, a visual learner who lacks perfect or relative pitch must read a piece of music repeatedly. He or she does not necessarily create an auditory pitch memory bank. Subsequently, these students cannot repeat the same piece of music after hearing or playing once or a few times. Instead, they rely only on their visual, tactile, or motor memory to digest the information. Memorization occurs only after repetitive playing.

Auditory Memory

What role does auditory memory play for students with absolute pitch? The ear dominates the learning process for those within the absolute pitch spectrum. When a student reads a simple melody line or hears a composition the first time, he or she automatically processes the piece in an auditory memory bank. By the second time he or she plays it, the piece has been largely learned via an auditory pathway (although the student *might not* be able to play it well).

Once this has happened, this auditory memory will compete with secondary learning mechanisms, including visual cues, sheet music, technical (finger) instruction, etc. Absolute pitch learners are often hindered by the interference coming from their auditory memory. Although these students may already "know" the music, they may not yet be able to play it. Further, they are often unable to integrate additional visual and physical cues that might help them master the music as they wish to play it.

On the other hand, the visual learner will read the music again and again without having the piece go into the auditory memory. Memorization only comes from repetitive playing.

Screening for Absolute Pitch

Few people can name musical pitches before they have begun studying an instrument. For children who are either too young to play an instrument or don't yet know how, observe these phenomena:

- Do they always sing on pitch?
- Do they try to harmonize?
- Are they obsessed or addicted to sound, or to creating and imitating rhythms?

Characteristic traits of students with absolute pitch or within the absolute-pitch spectrum:

- When thinking about a particular piece of music, the person hears a tape of the music playing in his or her head.
- When playing an instrument, he or she tries to match a certain melody to his or her particular instrument.
- The person gets easily annoyed when others sing along to a song, especially in confined spaces such as cars.
- The person displays excellent auditory rhythmic abilities and perceptions, and has an ability to perfectly emulate difficult auditory rhythms.
- The person has a gift for impersonation, or an ability to produce dead-on "pitch-perfect" imitations of accents, whether regional or foreign.
- The person can transpose a piece from one key to another instantaneously.
- The person can play a piece with his or her fingers without an instrument being present.
- The person hears and notes background noises that others without "sensitive hearing" might easily ignore. In a similar fashion, those with absolute pitch may make note of or be distracted by soft background music which other people seem not to notice, or are able to tune out.
- Despite a musical ability and an ability to read text, the person may be a poor visual reader of musical notation (or profess dyslexia when reading musical notation).
- The person can mentally practice a piece while doing another activity, and, as a result, can improve or enhance their musical performance.

- The person habitually rushes through music while playing.
- The person sets high goals for him or herself regarding music. Those goals are often unrealistic and impossible to achieve.
- When mistakes are made, the person tends to begin the piece over again.
- The person is tuned to a certain key, and plays or sings every piece in that key.
- The person is a multitasker in everyday life.
- The person displays an apparent lack of motivation in music lessons despite strong aptitudes.
- The person has an inner drive and motivation towards music, or is "addicted" to music.

To determine whether a student has absolute pitch by watching his or her behaviors:

- Does the student enjoy "picking out songs" on their instrument?
- When the student sings a particular song, does he or she always start it on a certain pitch?
- When the musical line goes too high or low for his or her voice, does the student jump up or down an octave in the middle of a musical line, to continue singing in the same key?
- Does the student have a strong sense of auditory rhythm?
- Can he or she imitate rhythm and pitch patterns?
- Can the student sing back or play a musical phrase after hearing it once?
- Does he or she harmonize while singing?
- Does the student cover his or her ears while you are trying to harmonize with them?
- Does the student revert to the original pitch when you try to change the key of a song?
- Does the student get easily frustrated when he or she is unable to play to his or her own standards of perfection?
- Does the student drop his or her head to look at his or her hands instead of reading the sheet music?

- Is the student tuned to a particular key, singing or playing every song in (for example) C or F or G?
- Does he or she act bored or inattentive when asked to play a piece of music for the second time?
- After making a mistake, does the student begin the piece over from the beginning of a line, or even from the beginning of the piece?

Screening for Relative Pitch

Always test for absolute pitch first. If the test fails, try the test for relative pitch, in which the student is given a pitch by name (and tone) and asked to provide the name of a pitch in relation to it. For those who are already learning an instrument, test as follows:

- Play a middle C and then another higher note in the same octave. Identify the middle C for the student, and have the student identify the second pitch.
- For example, play a "C" and ask your student, "If this is 'C,' then what is this note?" Then play a second note.
- If the student is unable to name the second note, have him or her try to match it on his or her own instrument.
- Repeat the test multiple times using a different second note each time. Continue playing middle C as the leading tone, but use a different second note each time. If the student correctly identifies most of the notes, they can be labeled as having relative pitch.

Minor errors with the test:

- After taking a break, the student may have trouble transitioning back into the learning mode. Thus results may be unreliable.
- The student must be familiar enough with the names of the notes to identify the keys correctly.

- By matching key to key, results are more consistent than when matching key to note name.
- Always test students on the instrument with which they are most comfortable. For example, if a student is learning the oboe, always test on an oboe. Testing a student on an instrument with which he or she is unfamiliar skews results.
- Children who are disabled might test inconsistently from week to week.

How to test for absolute pitch:

Always tell the student exactly how you will be testing for absolute pitch. Make sure he or she understands the process and is able to ask questions for clarification purposes.

For students who are already learning an instrument:

- Without allowing this student to look at you, play a note on the instrument he or she is most familiar with. Can the student name that note?

Hint: Avoid playing next-door neighbor tones, such as "C-D-E," etc. Instead, start with "G-C-E," etc.

- If the student is unable to complete this task, explain which set of notes you'll be using (the middle C position or a set of 5 consecutive keys). Then proceed to play a note without them looking at the tester's hands. Have the student match that note on their instrument. Do not tell them whether they are right or not.
- Repeat this process 5–10 times and see how many notes the student can match. Spread the testing sessions over several lessons, and test with different notes.
- A student can be labeled as having a skill within the spectrum of absolute pitch if he or she can correctly identify most of the notes.

Practical Application

Many complications can arise when someone unaware of the learning issues related to auditory perception teaches a student with absolute or relative pitch. If the student learns only auditorily, he might completely ignore the note-reading part of the lesson or try to "fake it" for his or her teacher, who might then feel that his or her instruction is being ignored. This can severely hinder progress in musical learning.

When auditory pitch processing dominates, a student might be able to play a piece by reading the notes the first time. Once the student hears himself play it, he may never read it again using full visual cues, and thus might never benefit from what the sheet music can add to his musical experience. Educators and therapists can benefit from the following responses to questions that we frequently get:

Q: I've determined that my student has perfect or relative pitch. How do I alter my teaching methods to suit his/her needs?

A: Begin by teaching *all* of your students as though they were auditory learners.

This creates less confusion once absolute or relative pitch is determined, and provides an appropriate structure for both visual and auditory learners.

- Never play a piece of music to your students before they have mastered the music.

Auditory learners will imitate what they hear, and become easily frustrated with their ability to duplicate the tones exactly. Playing a piece for a student stimulates their auditory memory but prevents them from playing the notes visually.

- Always use visual cues.

An auditory learner depends almost entirely on his or her ear to learn tones. Pointing to the written music is helpful because when auditory processing takes place, the student can find his or her place on the page when he or she looks up.

- Do not integrate the audio with visual skills until the visual skills are concrete.
- Do not entirely ignore auditory development. Strengthen it by doing purely auditory activities, including "playing by ear" without sheet music, and exercises in transposing by ear.
- By the same token, do not ignore developing visual skills. Strengthen them by doing purely visual activities. For example, when teaching a new piece, allow the student to read the music note for note independently the first one or two times they play it. This way, they absorb the music both visually and auditorily.
- Watch the student's eyes and see how much memorization is taking place. If the student is watching their hands a lot, this is a cue that they are processing the information auditorily.
- Teach visual letter names before teaching notes on a staff.

Have the student name the notes aloud once he or she can read them. This will ensure they are really reading them, rather than hearing the notes and then naming them from the pitch.

- Gradually teach left-hand chording when note skills are concrete. Then teach improvisation to keep the student interested.
- Play rhythm games on different instruments (i.e., percussion).
- Use absolute pitch skills to your advantage when giving commands. Often, by singing a command to a student instead of speaking it, the student comprehends better.

Will absolute pitch make a student a better musician? In many cases, absolute pitch is an advantage, particularly when a teacher is sensitive to its peculiar nature and educates students accordingly. By the same token, many of the world's best classical and jazz piano teachers are relieved when students *do not* have absolute pitch. These students are often thought to be more flexible and malleable, and teachers are more familiar with their learning mechanisms.

Does absolute pitch matter? What is the teacher's obligation to the student? Auditory and visual learners develop musical proficiencies differently. By balancing both styles of learning, new opportunities may open for students, music teachers, and music therapists.

Where repetition is vital to a visual learner, it's often destructive to an auditory learner. Music teachers and therapists who fail to recognize perfect and relative pitch, or who fail to modify their approach, also fail their students. For absolute pitch students, self-esteem is easily jeopardized.

As soon as a student is identified as having either absolute or relative pitch, it's important that the music teacher or therapist communicate this information to both the student and his or her parents. Often, absolute and relative pitch students carry over their auditory learning into the classroom. Parents can therefore bridge learning gaps at home and at school by understanding how their child learns.

Since auditory learners rely almost exclusively on their ears, students with absolute or relative pitch often avoid the obligation of learning to read music. Without that visual component, however, their progress is stunted, and they lack the foundation to study more advanced music. Ironically, the best teaching for a gifted auditory learner centers on visual cues and then builds on that.

Do absolute and relative pitch run in the family? An overwhelming majority of Susan's students with absolute or relative pitch report that the traits run in their families. Though many families encourage music, it seems likely that absolute and relative pitch also have a strong genetic component.

Some parents assume, incorrectly, that their child's disability is the reason he or she is musically gifted. In fact, any musical inheritance (and absolute and relative pitch skill) exists whether there is a disability or not. Upon recognizing the musical skills of a special-needs child, many families soon discover that siblings and other family members also have musical aptitude. Of Susan's testable absolute pitch students, fourteen out of fifteen reported that the phenomenon runs in their families, while eleven out of twelve students reported that relative pitch runs in their families. Similar results were found in the practice of another piano teacher in Susan's area, which prompted Henny to further investigate this phenomena.

Case Studies: Students with Absolute and Relative Pitch

Case Study 1: S is an eleven-year-old autistic boy. He is a strong-willed boy who tackles every task with intensity. For many years, he would fight, cry, and tantrum during lessons. Susan was very intent on teaching him to note read, and he is now doing it with ease. S displayed a great disconnect: He could not name the notes on the page and then find those notes on the keyboard. He is also a violent child, and his aggressive behaviors diminished as his note reading evolved. Now, he shows only perfect behavior in sessions and refers to note reading to learn—quite the change from the past. S used to despise practicing and he now practices consistently. He enjoys listening to movies and familiar shows and plays the scores that he imagines in his head. S is on auditory fire when asked to improvise with others, no matter the instrument.

Case Study 2: T is a six-year-old autistic boy. Due to difficulty with transitions he frequently head bangs, especially when arriving at sessions. Although head banging continued randomly, T just began note reading three sessions ago and now practices at home with an aide who knows piano. The head banging in sessions has nearly vanished. T now skips into the sessions, beaming with pride, and rushes to open his books to show off what he practiced all week. T tolerates Susan's touch to reposition his fingering. He is a very smart boy who will quickly grow into sight-reading to develop his technique and empower him in all areas of functioning.

A person with disabilities should study music with a music therapist so that the student's musical experience can be fully realized. Music therapists are specially trained to work with those who have special needs. In Susan's practice, a startling majority have absolute pitch. The special issues of Susan's students include autism, learning disabilities, genetic disorders, global delays, and Down syndrome. Susan also sees adults with various disorders. No matter how slight or invisible the special need, a music therapist should be consulted for best results.

Inquiries

Many times, strangers who are on their own personal journey of discovering their absolute pitch will send Susan a lengthy email, full of confusion, revelations, and questions. Susan also receives all kinds of feedback on her 2005 booklet and on her chapter in Dr. Treffert's book. Henny first connected with Susan after reading the chapter in Treffert's book. The following are typical transcripts of letters written to Susan:

Attila is a clarinetist, teacher, and doctoral student of psychology. He has absolute pitch and he loves to do sight-reading and improvising. He gets angry easily if somebody plays incorrectly or out of tune. He has extensive experience playing with the Debrecen Philharmonic Orchestra in Hungary.

October 26, 2012

Dear Susan:

After I read your booklet I realized that I have absolute pitch, too. I was never told that I had this capability, but I suspected.

When anyone asked me if I had absolute pitch, I answered "Maybe" or "Yes, but it is not complete." I have never known before that this capability is a spectrum, as Dr. Treffert said. My teachers realized that I am talented but I was never tested, and nobody tried to diagnose me. I could always benefit from it, especially at solfeggio lessons.

When I was a teenager, my friends often asked me to create ringtones to their mobile phones after hearing. It entertained me and my friends, who had not learned music and wondered how I could do that.

I have been writing some compositions since my childhood. In my early years, I did not have a piano, so I tried to write down the melodies in my head using my "inner hearing". I often hear melodies nowadays, but I rarely try to notice them.

Honestly speaking, I was delighted after I read your booklet and I recognized my giftedness, so I am grateful to you.

Yours sincerely,
Attila.

★ ★ ★

Emmy Award winner Stephen Lawrence composed 300 songs and scores for *Sesame Street*. Susan and Stephen met at Hava Nashira, a conference for Jewish musicians. After reading Susan's book, Stephen sent her the following letter:

June 3, 2008

Hi Susan,

I found your booklet very informative. Much of the material is consistent with my experience exactly although, as you might expect, some behavior that you describe does not coincide with my experience, as I will explain. And some patterns that were part of my early musical life are not covered in the booklet. They may be unique to me. For example, when I was learning a new piece in my pre-teens and teens, I always stopped short of learning the last couple of bars. This behavior was fairly consistent and I occasionally still must deal with it in my work. The difference is that as a professional composer who works with deadlines, I must finish on time. And I do. I have never delivered an assignment late. In April 2007, *Sesame Street* sent me 9 lyrics to set to music around the 20th of the month and gave me 10 days to deliver. I completed this work without much strain and some of it is among my favorite songs composed for the show.

Here are some patterns in my life, in no particular order, that are in agreement with your booklet and some that are not:

I do have a gift for imitating regional and foreign accents. Although I haven't done this for a few years, three or four years ago I spoke for periods lasting several days in British, Indian, Irish, and possibly other accents. I can't say how accurate I was, but I thought I sounded fairly accurate. It drove my family nuts.

I can play a piece with my fingers without needing an instrument.

Measured against the level at which I play the piano, my music-reading skills are lacking. I can sight-read fairly easy music but beyond that I'm much slower. I often cannot read without making mistakes with the inner voices when teaching my own arrangements to the singers of SATB scores written for my t'filah band.

Up until a few years ago, I often played my music for lyricists too fast. However, I do not play every song in the same key.

When I was much younger I might have preferred to play in C but now I generally can play songs in any key and am adept at transposing songs for singers. I usually do this by ear which is much faster for me than transposing written music with which I am less familiar.

I do not get annoyed when others sing along, except in theaters and when I am auditioning a new piece of music.

I experienced something at *Hava Nashira* that is new to me. In many classes, music was distributed and the song leader played it in a different key. In the past I could adjust and "make believe" the music was in the key in which it was played. But I found at Hava Nashira that it order to sing along I had to transpose in my head the written music.

If I make a mistake I do not need to return to the beginning of a song.

I did lack motivation in music lessons.

If my early piano teachers had not played a piece of music for me before I started to learn it I would have been forced to learn to read better.

"Do perfect and relative pitch run in the family?" Although my father was extremely talented musically (he did not become a professional), he did not have perfect pitch. He most definitely had relative pitch. My brothers and mother showed no special musical talent and we never thought to consider if they had perfect or relative pitch. Of course families go back beyond parents and siblings and it is quite possible that other family members possessed this ability.

I also lacked patience to practice. My frustration level was very high. So high that on one occasion I bit down hard on the keyboard cover and my tooth impressions were permanent.

I think music teachers would find the booklet a valuable tool in working with students with varying kinds and degrees of talent. It was a pleasure to speak with you during the days we were at *Hava Nashira*. I am not aware of anyone doing similar work.

Best wishes,
Stephen
StephenLawrenceMusic.com

Chapter Two

Absolute Pitch—
Why It Matters

Give me your gifted huddled masses yearning to breathe free.

Susan's clients sometimes come to her after bombing out with a traditional music teacher. As the struggles ensued, the teacher would blame the student, or his or her disabilities, when in fact the issue was the teacher not understanding the gift of absolute pitch. For the students, the disappointments, humiliation, and frustrations of the past created a dangerous association: all music instruction was awful, or the student was just plain stupid. The moment absolute pitch is addressed in Susan's music therapy sessions, disability flies out the window and learning can begin.

This is also true for musicians who struggle in college music programs. Only the best sight-readers have what it takes to survive the rigors of a conservatory. Often, the most gifted music makers can be found at improv groups, workshops, local bands, and talent shows.

These individuals are also most likely to have absolute pitch. Being forced to learn music visually might have turned them away from music training forever. There must be a tender balance between the visual and the auditory or the person will be stunted as a musician.

There is, however, a growing minority of people who cannot build a skill in an incremental manner. They master the geometry simply by seeing it or hearing it. The answer is there, they know it, but they can't tell you why. We call those individuals calendar-calculator savants. Then there are people who hear a piece of music one time and can play it back to you on their instrument. We call them musical savants.

But are they really savants, or is it absolute pitch showing you its amazing side? Well, it's a little of both. One might argue that being able to reproduce anything that you just heard is a savant ability. On the other hand, perhaps anyone is a genius if he or she can play some music that was just placed in front of him or her for the first time. It is just as easy for a left-brainer to sight-read music, as it is for a right-brainer to play what she just heard. In fact, the stronger the right-brain leanings are, the more intense that ability. On the other hand, that's how much more intense the inabilities are for that right-brainer to use left-brain functions. Most importantly, savants always have a developmental disability (e.g. autism, Down syndrome, etc.).

Prodigies and Savants

> *Music is a moral law. It gives soul to the universe, wings to the mind, flight to the imagination, and charm and gaiety to life and to everything.*
>
> —*Plato*

Music is primal. It isn't exclusively for a select elite. Every single human is wired to listen, appreciate, and interact with music. Music is any sound organized in time. It can be the simple whistling of a tune, or a complex eight-hour symphony.

Prodigies have a seemingly random burst of genius, while savants have (without training) overpowering inexplicable abilities alongside deep inabilities. Earning the title "musical savant" is like the Nobel Prize for the autistic. Henny refers to it as earning her tiara. A typically developed person is born with a brain that operates in its expected symmetrical manner. Speech will come from the brain's left side, visual processing from the occipital lobe in the back, music and language from the right brain. Such a person will be expected to do well in a typical classroom setting, and reach her developmental milestones in a continuous manner. At some point in her youth, she might join the school band and learn to play music.

What happens when such a typically developed person has exceptional abilities? For a dedicated student who masters her instrument with great proficiency, the skill is a testament to her diligence. The longer she works at it, the faster she can decipher the notes and create sound. But what about those who've never been taught about those dots on the page? They should not be able to enter the world of creating music, correct? But we know about the great masters who have brought us amazing music without ever having learned to read music.

Creating sound is primal. All humans yearn to connect through a medium that transcends the spoken word. Rhythm is the first language that we are exposed to through the maternal heartbeat in utero. When we are born, we are ready to continue that pulse. As the infant develops, his musical abilities become enriched. In Piaget's sensorimotor stage, from birth to two years, babies can distinguish pitches and seek out their source. This is the incredible capacity of the human brain. Even individuals who fail to reach certain developmental milestones after that can still process, interact, reciprocate, and create through music.

Dr. Darold Treffert defines a savant as an individual who has his or her special ability superimposed and grafted onto an underlying disability. A prodigy, on the other hand, has some special, conspicuous, and sometimes prodigious ability that exists in the absence of an underlying disability. There are three types of savants: Splinter skill savants, prodigious savants, and acquired savants. Typically, autistic individuals will begin to demonstrate their splinter skills early in life through their special interests, or as "Islands of Ability" (Treffert, *Extraordinary People: Understanding Savant Syndrome*).

Prodigious savants have an inexplicable and exceptional mastery in something specific. A photographic or auditory memory is always present in the extremely narrow and limited-range savant types. Eidetic memory is a vivid recall process for color images to persist in the visual field after scanning an object (Treffert, *Extraordinary People*, p. 16).

Merriam-Webster defines *prodigy* as a highly talented child or youth, yet savants are defined as persons of learning, especially those with detailed knowledge in some specialized field. The exceptional gift is the astounding ability in savants. A young child who possesses the glories of the gift on top of his or her *typical* development is a prodigy. An acquired savant is a typically developed individual who inexplicably displays a prodigious ability after a traumatic injury.

Savant ability can exist in individuals with typical development. The 1887 term "idiot savant" has been dissolved, and "savant syndrome" is now the proper diagnostic term for an individual with savant abilities, with or without accompanying disabilities. In autistic individuals, savant abilities are very profound in contrast with apparent weaknesses, which makes them outstanding examples of this label. Susan finds that very rarely do parents recognize that their child is a savant until she brings it to their attention.

Savants have abilities that should be nurtured by a professional who understands how to do that. "It is through those extraordinary abilities that the savants speak to us. It is their language, and for some at first, their only language."[6] This intricate work is demanding of the teacher but also very rewarding for all involved. Throughout this book,

---

[6] Treffert, Darold, "My Marvelous Journey with Incredible Savants: What Have I Learned?" *Scientific American*, July 31, 2013

techniques for the extreme learner are integrated within the regular method. The system is the same, no matter the level of ability. Absolute pitch is a spectrum, and as soon as one meets that criterion, his needs become the same as the extreme learner's. If the correct method is used, the teacher then progresses at the student's speed. The formula remains intact, no matter the speed or extremes of the student. This is about process, not product. The goal is to work through the process rather than spit out a weekly performance.

Absolute Pitch is Not a Curse

Susan often quips to the naysayers, "The only curse with absolute pitch is that you don't have it." Rather than blame absolute pitch for learning differences, one should use the assessment of AP to determine how the individual learns best.

In a musical manner, testing for AP is the easiest and fastest way to test for a learning style, which gives a clue to the person's brain wiring in about ninety seconds. All other learning-style assessment methods take much longer and are costlier. Of course, this does not replace expert neuropsychology tools applied by qualified clinicians; it's only a tool to empower the educator when first seeing a new student and learning how to best meet their needs.

Students with AP who have never touched an instrument before will have a very specific behavior when first observed at the piano: They exhibit the desperate hunted-animal look as they clamor and stumble to get that sound out from inside their heads. AP'ers have the sound permanently etched into their auditory memories after having heard it just once, but because their technique isn't yet refined, they can't get it out fast enough. This is the first sign to observe for absolute pitch before beginning an assessment for an untrained possessor.

Average piano teachers won't teach children younger than age eight because they can't get the kids to sit on the piano bench long enough. Susan accepts students of all ages, and will start teaching piano usually at age four. In Susan's music therapy sessions, kids will commit to the hard work, knowing they get "free play" afterward. The first thing the client does is walk in and start to play the piece assigned the week before. The next piece is then explored together, and the work is done. For the younger students, this usually takes about ten to fifteen minutes. They are then given a choice of what to do next. Because these students often have AP, they excel at the work but also crave musical free play. Improvisation is their strength, and their rhythm and singing skills can be observed during that time. Ordinarily, the classically trained piano teacher won't have that opportunity.

In this way, the strengths are evident right from the start. The student is also acknowledged, as their parents can begin to see the greater dimensions of the whole child. When they are diagnosed with absolute pitch, it begins to make sense to the parents. They can now observe the entire phenomenon from every angle of strength. The student and caregivers should be informed and educated on this, and they need to be reminded to tell the world, so that the student can be revered in society. Young students who reveal their gift to their band teacher or classmates begin to see an immediate turnaround in the level of respect they receive—a respect that they didn't even have to do anything to get! This is fabulous for self-esteem, even in the absence of disabilities or learning challenges.

Absolute pitch is like a flower: It keeps blooming, and at different times, different qualities emerge. Some kids are able to sight-sing early on; for others it takes a longer time. Some children can look at a chord and hear it. Some can accompany on a *djembe* with exceptional rhythm, including dynamics and cadences. Validating these abilities throughout this progress is like giving them "gifts."

Let's examine the case of Paul, who first came to Susan as a fourteen-year-old back in the early 1980s. Paul was learning guitar and piano, and doing very well. Labeled severely autistic but functionally verbal, he needed supervision all the time because of the strange things he would get himself into. Paul was truly a savant with exceptional musical ability.

Paul's mother was very dedicated and supportive. Paul was a joy to teach because his ear was so good. Susan's living room served as a waiting area at the time. There was a toy chest full of toys, and bookshelves for children to occupy themselves while waiting for their session. One day, Paul picked up the Fisher-Price See 'n Say toy and took it into the bathroom with him. The toy has a bright yellow arrow, which can be spun to point at an animal. The toy then plays the appropriate recording to make the matching animal's sound.

When Paul's session time arrived, his mother went to the bathroom to retrieve him. That was when she discovered that he had the toy with him but had completely immersed it in water. When questioned, he responded matter-of-factly, "I wanted to hear the 'glub glub glub' in the water." An outsider would observe this as autistic behavior, or the behavior of an individual with an intellectual disability, but for an absolute-pitcher, it's classic. Given that the ear has a desperate craving for sound, anything in the environment becomes an opportunity to experience a sound whose harmoniousness is greater than the sum of its parts. "Glub glub glub" is a funny sound, certainly pleasing to a perfect-pitch ear, but imagine that sound with the waves of water added and you can have a symphony with many harmonies. Of course, a non-possessor would struggle to hear the nuances of those microtones, but an absolute-pitcher can imagine them without submerging the toy, and still experience delight from audiating the possibilities inside his head.

Visual Processing Challenges

Vision acuity and visual perception are not interchangeable. Just because you see something does not mean you can necessarily identify what it is you are seeing. For people with visual distortions, seeing letters on a page (and even reading them), is easy. But understanding what they read is an entirely different function. William Padula, an OD, defines vision as "a dynamic, interactive process of motor and sensory function mediated by the eyes for the purpose of simultaneous organization of posture, movement, spatial orientation, manipulation of the environment, and, to its highest degree, perception and thought."

Visual processing problems such as convergence insufficiency, hyperopia, and saccadic insufficiency are never observed in a standard eye exam. If parents have had their child tested annually, they have only the information on vision acuity. Experts in visual processing can further evaluate whether the brain is actually making sense of what the individual is looking at. Processing disorders can be noticed in the following ways:

- Individual tends to cock his head.
- Peers from corner of his eyes.
- Has difficulty making eye contact.
- Avoids looking at anything nearer than arm's-length.
- Appears to lose focus; isn't listening to directions.
- Squints, contorts face, flickers fingers near eyes, covers eyes, closes one eye.
- Claims to see better with the lights dimmed.
- Prefers printed material on colored pages.
- Appears to struggle to read, even with enlarged print.
- Complains of headaches, throbbing in and around eyes, temples, and/or top of head.
- Rubs eyes; has stinging, watery, red eyes.
- Fatigues easily when reading or performing near-vision activities such as writing with a pen, threading a needle, adjusting fingerings on a guitar neck.
- Complains of seeing double.
- Has difficulty climbing or descending stairs; holds on to railing for dear life, and scopes out the next step with one foot first.
- Fears sudden changes in height, such as sitting down on a chair.
- Suddenly reads with fluidity when colored filters are placed over written material.
- Feels sick to her stomach after reading.
- Experiences motion sickness when riding in a car.
- Complains of after-shadows hovering above images long after looking at a brighter object.
- Reports that letters are dancing, swimming, jumping, moving, flickering, or walking over each other.

- Looks up and away from her fingers, especially when playing an instrument.
- Will flick a crumb off of his shirt while looking away.

Until an expert corrects these issues through treatment, the following temporary accommodations can be made:

- Use audio textbooks.
- Assign preferred classroom seating, such as front-left, to allow the individual to use his right eye only.
- Dim the lights to reduce contrast.
- Experiment with a sans-serif and also a serif typeface to add or remove the fine cross-stroke found at the top and/or bottom of a letter in some fonts.
- Place colored filters over written material.
- Draw the window shades in the room.
- Cover all bright objects such as computer and charger-cable lights.
- Cover one eye for short durations if reading is a must.
- Frequent breaks.
- Wearing sunglasses.
- Use Irlen lenses, filters prescribed by an Irlen expert.
- Encourage the individual to step on the sidewalk lines to feel her next step.
- Schools can accommodate, just as a blind student would be accommodated.
- (The accommodations listed above are not helpful for those who need vision therapy.)

If the person's eyes do not converge, the eyes will remain fixed in the position for seeing something from afar, and he or she will therefore be unable to see written material in front of her. The brain gets two separate images and tries to put them together, but fails. This is extremely painful, fatiguing, and nauseating. A specialist can easily assess the severity of the processing disorder.

By labeling it "extreme right-brain," we can offer an explanation as we further explore this subject. The majority of individuals with very high levels of AP are using extreme right-brain functions to learn, process, store, and recall information. This brain wiring neglects left-brain strengths such as math and reading comprehension. Our vision must use left- and right-brain processing to give us the complete picture. Establishing that your student has a left- or right-brain variation of AP is key to understanding his or her strengths.

Right-brained AP'ers have specific asymmetry with visual processing. Even with 20/20 vision, they can be nearly "blind" to understanding what they're seeing. Most people manage to get by without knowing what their issue is, and make it into adulthood by hovering just above failure. Younger children who struggle on very high levels are at risk of being misdiagnosed with learning disabilities. In reality, all they need is eye exercises from a neuro-ophthalmologist who specializes in perceptual disorders.

Eye exercises begin to strengthen the visual processing, which forms neural connections to the neglected hemispheres. For younger children, these exercises can be boring or even painful because there's no motivation. Adults might value the end result as they see their abilities improve from week to week.

As the individual struggles through sight-reading music, two things occur: First, his or her left-brain functions begin to be used, painfully at first, and then his or her overall visual processing improves. Throughout this process, all areas of functioning benefit, even if learning an instrument was the sole intention.

This result has been documented from observation of nearly 400 people. The magic occurs when one has been sight-reading for 30 percent of his or her life. For young children, this is not a long time. There's a catch, though: People with AP tend to scan the melody without really reading it because it's so difficult to decipher what the notes are without the left-brain functions of figure-ground extraction. Therefore they fake it, fooling even themselves. At times, their abilities are so remarkable that it can be years before any teacher realizes that his or her student actually can't read music.

That's why this book stresses the vital importance of assessing for AP. You want to know what's going on with the individual so you know what to work with. By knowing the type of AP he or she has (left- or right-brained), you can determine what his or her strengths are. This book explains how to teach for these variations. The teaching is designed to use the strengths while bridging the brain connections to the areas of weakness. For individuals with AP, the sound that emerges from the instrument when they read the music is motivating enough for them to plow through it.

Unlike eye exercises, this specific technique for teaching with the Rancer Method will get the most challenged student playing by reading music, with steady progress in every area of life. Offering colored charts, stickers, or fake-sheets directly adapts to the weakness. The eye-tracking and visual-processing improvements can't begin before sight-reading is incorporated.

The classical notation system has been around for hundreds of years. Throughout history, the aural tradition was too challenging to carry on to the next generation, so laws, traditions, and music have been written down for the benefit of the offspring. Music history is very much a part of our culture, and understanding the notation and the theory is necessary for learning it. Every human being is owed the dignity of being taught how to use music to communicate with the world in a widely understood lingo. On a simpler level, knowing how to sight-read provides more opportunities for connecting with others, and makes music more accessible to all. Unlike just listening to music, sight-reading opens up both channels of the brain so that the ears and the eyes can work together for optimal learning.

Reading Comprehension and Eye Movement

The overlap between clumsiness, depth perception, eye movement, and reading comprehension is significant. Accommodation and convergence insufficiencies of vision and visual processing difficulties are very simple to test and diagnose, but go unnoticed in most people for a lifetime. This is because your annual eye exam tests only how well you see the letters on the wall so your optometrist can adjust your prescription. To this day, Henny tests as 20/20 (and higher) in those eye exams, but struggles with her vision in many ways.

Often, a student will be diagnosed with a learning disability such as dyslexia, or labeled as having a reading disability or ADHD. In essence, these kids have tremendous stamina, as they endure countless hours of pain while trying to see printed material through visual distortions.

Imagine if the letters in this book suddenly began to separate into two pictures. You're now seeing double; however, your brain knows that it shouldn't be seeing two images, so it fights to combine them. As you focus on the letters and become unsure about which one to use and which to ignore, you begin to see the two images float into each other. The images will bob, dance, hit each other, and bounce back into two pictures again. This constant movement can result in motion sickness. Students who complain about their eyes hurting might also complain that they get dizzy, see spots, and feel nauseated, lightheaded, or fatigued after trying to read for a minute. The longer one fights to read through these symptoms, the faster the motion sickness begins to kick in.

Depending on the severity of the disorder, the eyes will begin to refuse to accommodate to near-vision tasks. Also, many people might have Irlen Syndrome, a visual processing problem where the brain cannot accommodate to near-vision tasks. In many cases, the issues carry over into the area of depth perception, and the individual might appear to be clumsy or terrified of heights, stairs, or moving objects such as cars, swings, or Grandma's lap.

Henny has been asked many times, "how can you drive?" She is quick to joke, "Oh, I am the safest driver on the road. I avoid double as many cars as you." Realistically, her vision is perfectly fine, and she is a very safe driver. Practically, she has major issues with understanding what she sees. Here is a recent anecdote of her experience:

> Last week, I went to the dentist for a 7:00 am appointment. I purchased two hours in the parking meter, and placed the receipt on my dashboard. When

I returned an hour later, there was a parking ticket on my dashboard. I was really upset because I still had another hour of parking paid for, and now I would have to go contest this ticket, wasting my time and energy. When I arrived to the traffic violations office, they told me that the code on the ticket was for a violation in "wrong way-1 way or 2 way." That is when it hit me. As I was pulling out from my parking spot, other drivers were honking at me. I made a u-turn and left that street, not realizing I had parked on a 1-way street, but facing the wrong direction. Yes, I saw the car in front of me parked, and I neatly lined my car up. Although I saw the object, I didn't connect the image to the understanding that it was facing me, and therefore I was incorrect. This is not a typical occurrence, as I have learned that my processing is slowed in times of distress, overload, or in this case, an early morning trip to a dentist appointment.

At a recent evaluation with an eye specialist, Henny was administered a Tangent Screen for visual field testing. The patient peers through a device elevated above a dark board, and fixates their eyes on the center point of the board. The doctor holds a baton with a colored tip, and moves it slowly from the corners of the board toward the center. When the patient recognizes the color of the baton tip, they call out the color. The doctor then marks the spot on the board where the patient's awareness came into focus. Henny failed spectacularly on this test. Although she was able to see that there was a color, her brain did not reveal the associated name for the color until it was right in the center of the board. This uncomfortable and even panicky feeling can make anyone feel incredibly stupid and disabled. Henny says, "I felt like I was going crazy. It's like my brain was seeing but unable to extract the data from the image. It felt like I was in a dream where I couldn't move my legs."

Henny did not have vision therapy as a child, and her vision has deteriorated to the extent that she now identifies as having a visual impairment. An individual might as well be considered visually impaired since his or her eyes are of no help in navigating the world and performing the basic tasks necessary for daily living and academia.

First, you want to discontinue whatever is causing pain. For untreated students, that might be everything you're trying to teach in the lesson. Next, you want to find ways to accommodate the student while they begin vision-training therapy.

Henny survived college by being accommodated in creative ways:

> I got my prism glasses only in the last seven weeks before graduating. What I did was use the Finale software. The screen was set to a pale antique yellow and thin gray staff lines. The notes were black. The most painful for me are half notes, and only when the thickness of the circle outline is the same thickness as the staff line that it sits on. I can't distinguish between the note and the line, so if the staff lines are *very* thin and gray, it makes them fade in the distance and be less threatening to my eye. I end up imagining the lines, and judge the notes by the intervallic/spatial relationships, one to the next. Also, setting the screen to scroll view rather than page view allows me to keep my eye in the center of the screen without having to jump to the next system. Otherwise I'd be unable to find my place and would have to start laborious eye tracking for each new system. That would be every four measures! With the scroll view, the computer does the work, and my eyes remain still.

Braille requires a "touch-to-translate" concept, which is a processing inability most often found in people who already have a convergence insufficiency and accommodation disorder. The trick is to hook the student into playing right away, and then polish up her technique and rhythm. After several months, it becomes time to transition into note reading with the least amount of effort. When Henny was fitted for Irlen Spectral filters on top of her prism glasses, she had the following experience:

> I went to a local Irlen diagnostician for testing today for Irlen Spectral Filters. In the process, different tints of plastic are placed over the eyes. The idea is to find a combination of several layers that calm the vision enough to have better processing. I had extreme reactions to the tints. The simple task of removing one color and adjusting to the new color brought on waves of nausea, but not all the time. Some colors were like a warm fuzzy blanket after a near-drowning hypothermia situation. I had excruciating pain for any color that had hints of blue, red, or yellow. This meant that the browns were not suitable for me, and the purples and oranges were out too. The black/grey and pure greens were my balm. I settled on a six-tint combo and am awaiting that new pair to arrive soon.
>
> Here's what's interesting: Inside my head, I felt a distinct tug/pull in certain regions from behind the eye, all the way to the back. It was on the left side. The diagnostician said that many with Synesthesia have reported this. These pulls happened in a different "lane" depending on the color. I was able to predict where it would hurt just by knowing that we were now trying a certain color group. Here's a diagram of the three colors I felt (I couldn't feel any others):

Visual information goes from the eye to the brain to be processed and interpreted.

When the assessment was complete, I took a walk outside the room with the Irlen colored lenses clipped to my glasses. For the first time in my life, the floor was deathly cold and silent. I knew where to put my feet to get to the other side. It was almost disorienting to see the other office doors coming closer and closer to me, like a video simulation of a car-racing game. When I got to the end of the hallway, there was a staircase. I realized that for the first time in my life, I knew where the hallway ended, and I wasn't touching the wall to know that information. Every step was clearly marked and I was able to imagine how I'd get to the bottom without having to listen for the sound of my footsteps, or feeling out the edges of each step with my feet. Most importantly, back in the room, I used my Irlen Spectral Filters with the glasses to peer between the bookshelves on the right side and left side of the room. None of the books were dancing around, the gilded binders were not screaming, and everything was mellow and silent. Gone were the inner waves of agony when moving my eyes rapidly from side to side. Even if this was a placebo or witchcraft, I was eternally grateful for the relief I was experiencing.

Chapter Three

Right Brain/Left Brain Learning Traits

You might have heard people say, "Oh, I'm such a left-brainer," or "She's that right-brain creative type." Right-brainers (RB) and left-brainers (LB) are distinctly different in every area of functioning, and these traits are magnified with those who possess absolute pitch.

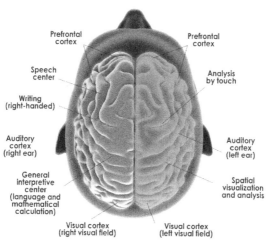

Brain functions by hemisphere.

LBAP/RBAP: Henny's Variations Theory

Absolute pitch presents in two stark variations, with a spectacular middle ground. Henny identifies these variations as left-brain absolute pitch (LBAP) and right-brain absolute pitch (RBAP). The practical application of identifying the variations is to predict learning strengths and weaknesses without first having to assess for reading comprehension, math, and other learning disabilities. Of course, this does not replace the expert neuropsychology tools of qualified clinicians; this is only a tool to empower the educator when first meeting a new student and learning how to best meet her needs from the start.

Our interest in brain variations first began with Susan's observation of her clients. Some of them consistently displayed great trouble and frustration with sight-reading, despite years of training. Further discussion with their parents revealed similar struggles with schoolwork. Upon in-depth exploration of the exact nature of the difficulty, we were able to narrow it down to a visual/auditory processing and convergence issue.

This led to a research endeavor on understanding how different brains process information differently, leaving the individual with major challenges. The goal was to discover how one learns, and in turn know how best to teach to those preferred learning styles. The first step began with our studies on how all clients processed information. Observing this, we recognized some distinct variations, which revealed a delightful discovery.

We tested musically trained musicians, many with PhDs, alongside preverbal, nonverbal, and non-musically trained individuals for Absolute pitch. Not surprisingly, years of training did not correlate with AP, meaning those who had college degrees in music still did not have AP. In fact, less than half of the musically trained individuals tested had it, yet with our autistic subjects, all except for one (97 percent) had AP, whether they were verbal or not.

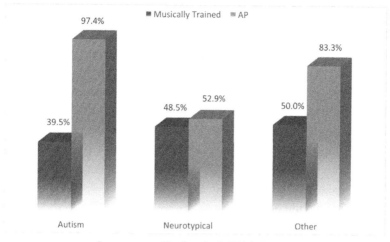

Image source: Kupferstein & Walsh (2015)

By testing with piano-pitch matching rather than note naming, we eliminated the bias in the research against those with language differences. Further, this opened up the study to more observable traits that helped us formulate the RB/LB distinctions. For example, subjects were also asked to improvise, to compose, transpose, play from note reading, or play from memory.

RBAP vs. LBAP Assessment

The following table resulted from a survey of Susan's clients and of musicians who were tested for AP and answered Henny's questions about their LB/RB traits.

- At least six markers are needed to identify a variation.
- Sight-reading for more than 30 percent of one's life creates a morph of RB+LB, considered a success story.

	RBAP	LBAP
1	Poor reading comprehension	Excellent reading comprehension
2	Poor math logic	Excellent math logic
3	Struggles to sight-read music.	Sight-reads very efficiently.
4	Sight-reads by hovering over melody line and imagining pitches that could belong in with that sound. Dim lighting makes the staff lines fade so that the melody line is starker.	Sight-reads by calculating interval spacing. Bright lighting makes the intervals stand out better for calculation.
5	Eye tracks up and down, hunting out each pitch separately; gets lost as they pick apart the piece trying to make sense of the sound, one pitch at a time. Gets tripped up by inversions and passing tones that don't "belong."	Eye tracks the whole sequence of the entire measure, both clefs simultaneously, understanding the logic of the entire piece by looking at the score. Recognizes inversions visually.
6	Must play the piece with full orchestration as heard. Will also throw in the embellishments such as trills, and bridge sections.	Can do an instant reduction by extracting soprano and bass lines only.
7	Hates Bach or contrary motion; complains that there is no melody to latch on to. May refer to the sound as awful, mechanical, painful, horrible.	Loves Bach because it makes mathematical sense. Identifies the logic by analyzing the whole sequences. May say of the music, "it all makes sense," "it's brilliant."

8	Craves to play something they just heard and liked the sound of. While relishing the process of hunting and pecking, they never play it again once they've completely reproduced it. The fascination is with the process of creating the product.	Craves to have the logic all thought through, and only then enjoys the high of replaying it once they've cracked the code. The fascination is with the end product itself.
9	Keeps eyes and ears as close to the sound source as possible.	Organized posture to visually take in all the musical notes and keys at the same time.
10	In the autistic population, the rocking of the bench symbolizes the sound not coming out fast enough from inside the auditory perception/processing/memory.	In the NT (Neuro-Typical) population, the physical posture is memorized so that arms and fingering are the same when learning to play, and later, when performing.
11	May refer to sections as "where the yellows turn to green," or "where the birds fly away."	May refer to sections as "where my shoulder tenses," or "where my hands have to cross over."
12	When sight-reading, eyes are all over the place, back and forth between notes and fingers, desperate to visualize the sound.	When sight-reading, eyes remain in a perfect straight line, never veering from the notes.
13	Gets lost even if the teacher points to the music.	Ignores the teacher's pointing, keeps going on his own.

14	Imitates voices of characters in movies, or imitates household sounds	Is not intrigued by sounds just heard; gravitates to reproducing already stored or formal sound from previous lessons.
15	Memorizes a piece by playing it as far as he can go from auditory memory, using the sheet music as a last resort reference.	Memorizes by looking at the sheet music and playing it over and over, until the fingers can do it with his eyes closed.
16	Might melt down when music is placed in front of her and instructed, "Now play."	Might melt down if you take the music away from her and instruct, "Now play."
17	To make a call, he enters the phone number by knowing the "song" of the number rather than the individual numerals. Recites the melody or demonstrates dialing fingers when prompted. Can hear a wrong number dialed without realizing which number he pressed. (Mostly generational, children of the '80s)	Knows telephone numbers by heart, reciting the numbers when prompted. Thinks that knowing the song of a telephone number is weird, or cool.
18	Feels desperately lost when a telephone or calculator keypad is in a different order.	Can effortlessly dial numbers regardless of the keypad order.
19	Refers to detailed information with qualitative associations such as "when we lived in the green house" instead of "in 2003."	Refers to detailed information in quantitative associations such as "twelve years ago," using logic to compute.

20	When prompted to improvise, will need just a spark, such as a theme, to set her off to create something wondrous.	When prompted to improvise, will refer to already known music, and alter a detail by shifting the sequence around to produce a different sound for it.
21	When transposing, will use just the pointer fingers, or cross fingers sloppily; as production of the sound in the head takes center stage, fingering and technique falls to the wayside.	When transposing, will shift entire hand to new placement by calculating where the starting and ending point would be in another key, using scale degrees.
22	Attacks a transposing challenge with glee. Might ask for more such challenges.	Regards a transposing challenge as a boring/non-stimulating chore, unless she has a very prodigious form of LBAP.
23	Can merge styles of limitless music selections, such as "play Beethoven's 9th symphony in blues style." Loves figuring it out; plays in real-time while processing it aurally.	Can merge styles only after calculating it quietly in their heads, silently tapping out the fingers. Will play it only after it is thought through.
24	Would give up a limb to be able to play 24/7.	Would consider it a bore when asked to play a new pop tune by ear.
25	Must read books aloud to process aurally and derive meaning.	Reading aloud does not help or make a difference. Can understand just by reading once.

26	Must read in a quiet, dark place to take in the fewest visual and auditory stimuli.	Can read anywhere; extraneous stimuli do not interfere. Might even enjoy listening to music while reading.
27	Can have a permanent auditory memory.	Can have a permanent visual memory.
28	Can point out where in the music you are playing, after hearing it once.	Can watch your fingers to see the sequence of your progressions to map their way through the code and then find it on the sheet music.
29	Looks up and away when playing from auditory memory. Hums the next pitch to remember the next pitch.	Scrutinizes the keys, plays from visual memory and recites the letter names of the next sequence.
30	When he detects a mistake in the playing, he goes back to the beginning of the phrase or the beginning of the piece.	Might not detect a mistake, but if he does, he will redo the same part or back up only to the start of that measure.
31	Will beg, bargain or melt down when asked to start playing from a certain point in the middle of a piece. Does not know where in the song you are if you play a random measure.	Can play from any given point without effort. Considers it redundant to repeat a whole section if she already knows the opening part well.

32	Skips notated dynamics when playing the first time. Can insert dynamics and infuse their playing with musicality only after having played it through once.	Can play the notated dynamics as written the first time reading it, but often lacks the musicality for interpretation of the phrasing.
33	Does not understand why inversions are necessary or are even considered chords. Sticks to chords in root position until they prove to themselves that inverted chords make it easier to navigate the keyboard.	Loves the value of inverted chords, saying it makes his playing so much easier.

Once the auditory style is identified as RBAP, educators can design their teaching practice so as not to burn out the student by forcing a traditional approach. The next layer is to use the strengths of the RBAP while integrating the left brain. This is done with the Rancer Method, so that the ear falls to the wayside while visual processing strengthens. Simultaneously, this provides the auditory feedback that the RBAP craves so much. This is a rewarding method to stimulate the visual processing because it's more enjoyable than going to a clinic and doing eye exercises. After all, when creating sound is motivating to the ear, practicing eye exercises loses its appeal, especially if they're painful.

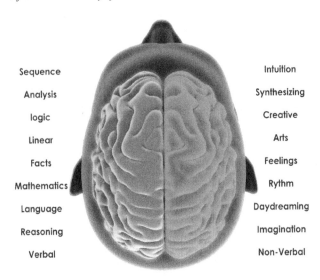

Brain process by hemisphere side.

Individuals who are right-brainers and also have AP will struggle with math, reading comprehension, and note reading. In a study that involved brain imaging, Dr. Fumiko Hoeft, a cognitive neuroscientist and psychiatrist at the University of California, San Francisco, explains how reading comprehension and speech are related in reading-comprehension struggles. Reading ability originates in the left temporoparietal lobe, where phonological processing, speech, and reading begin the neural journey in linking sounds and letters and how they correspond. Hoeft discovered that strong white-matter pathways are a predictor of greater neural activation in the right prefrontal cortex, which accounts for greater phonological achievements in tasks tested.[7] This prediction of literacy and language skills is critical for understanding why students with overarching right-brain strengths will struggle with left-brain tasks.

---

[7] Myers, C. A., Vandermosten, M., Farris, E. A., Hancock, R., Gimenez, P., Black, J. M., et al. (2014). White matter morphometric changes uniquely predict children's reading acquisition. *Psychological science,* 25(10), 1870-1883.

An increase in white matter can prompt the activity in the pathways underutilized from right brain to left brain. In the environment of music education, it's crucial to design the tasks in a sequence that will prompt these changes in brain development. For example, the moment the student looks at the book more than he looks at his fingers, you can begin to see how the change is occurring. As the lessons progress, the student shows sustained eye tracking because his fingers already trust that they are in position, and each finger is in charge of a different key. Without looking at his hands, the motor response is now activated to the visual stimuli. Previously, the student relied on his ear to know that he had played, because he heard it. Now, he knows he played because he felt his finger depressing. For those with sensory integration issues, this is even more profound when the keyboard has weighted keys. The tactile input is key for training the brain not to rely on the ear for feedback on movement. Thus begins the journey of brain training through this method.

It is typical to see a student do well in the first lesson because the songs are printed with letter names only. The first few songs are composed with no skips or leaps, and the fingers play in the order of the scale, which sets the student up for success. In the third song, however, the test pushes the limits of the untrained brain. The first gigantic leap is right there in the opening of the song. The student has to figure out how to go from C to F. This is the moment when the barriers dissolve, and it becomes obvious to the teacher that for the sake of creating music, the student will do whatever it takes. One adult student exclaimed, "Ouch, I can feel my brain sizzling" as she tried to play it without looking at her hands. Others sweat from exertion. Still, the brain training has begun.

They all figure it out. Some take longer, while others fly through the method book in a week. No matter the pace, the progression of skill builds critical pathways, and the foundation is then set for sophisticated learning. In Henny's practice, non-verbal students are encouraged to sing the letter names while playing, as well as the lyrics of the songs they play. It's not unusual for a student to begin vocalizing in the lesson for the first time in her life. For Henny, this is merely an indicator that the connections are being made.

Many of Henny's students recently had such breakthroughs quite early in their training. One twelve-year-old nonverbal student chose to replace the lyrics of his assigned piece at his fourth lesson, and sang it while playing. A five-year-old nonverbal student discovered his voice in the second month of training. As his sounds were played back for him on the piano, his face lit up as if to say, "Wait—you guys actually know what I'm thinking? Wow! Let me try this again." And more and more sounds emerged, until a musical conversation was exchanged. Another student, a 14-year-old girl with a passion for Jewish music, pointed to a letter board (RPM method) to demonstrate that she knows the translation of the Hebrew words of the song that she just sang along to with Henny. All of these communication breakthroughs occurred even before the introduction of note-reading.

Success Stories

The LBAP/RBAP morph success stories are all of individuals who've been sight-reading long enough so that their reading comprehension and math emerge to the extent that they can survive academically. Though not all are excelling in those areas, they're no longer failing. This is the happy medium we seek to accomplish for right-brain AP'ers who need help bringing the left brain into the picture when logic is needed to process formulaically instead of aurally. A 4-year-old child will only need 18 months (30% of her lifetime) of lessons with the Rancer Method to see these results.

T is a fifteen-year-old male with perfect pitch. He can name guitar chords perfectly and composes extensively. He has been note reading for more than eight years, which is 58 percent of his lifetime. He is doing very well academically, and is good in math and reading comprehension.

N, an eighteen-year-old female, is a voice major in college. She is a right-brained absolute pitcher and has a terrible time in math and reading comprehension. Though she has had the lead role in the school's opera production, she continues to coast by in other classes. N is able to cope academically because she was introduced to sight-reading when she was in fifth grade.

E, a nineteen-year-old male, is a piano major in college. He has many markers to be classified as a right-brained perfect pitcher, but is good in math and reading comprehension. He loves to compose, and hates playing Bach. E has been sight-reading for most of his life. As a result, he's doing very well in all coursework.

J is an 8-year-old autistic boy. He has been receiving music therapy for three years. Additionally, he has also done extensive eye exercise and interactive metronome therapy. He no longer loses his spot when reading, and no longer needs to have someone point to find the musical notes on the page. He has also gained tremendous finger strength and hand-eye coordination. He can handle math problems if introduced to him in chunks.

Y is a 52-year-old college professor with a Ph.D. in Biology. As a scientist, she is intrigued by genetics, because of "the beauty in the patterns". She is an RBAP who has been introduced to note-reading as a young child (92% of her lifetime). She adamantly fought the note-reading, and instead, improvises and composes extensively. As a result, she has an awful time with math and reading comprehension.

Chapter Four

Why Start With Piano?

> *You can fool the fans, not the players [because they might have absolute pitch].*
>
> —John Cage

While awaiting the birth of their child, every couple goes through the same fantasy: They lie in bed and tell each other, "Our child is going to study the piano." The moment they receive a diagnosis of autism or any disability, all those dreams vanish. In the grieving process, parents struggle to come to terms with everything that, according to the clinicians, their child will never be able to do.

As their child develops and begins to defy expectations, parents are afraid to hope, as they face the burden of potentially overpowering inabilities. Day after day, week after week, they attend staff meetings, individualized education plan (IEP) meetings, and school staff discussions about what isn't working for their child. After consulting with Susan or Henny, they learn that depending on the age and developmental level, piano study is indeed in their child's future.

After starting music sessions, suddenly their child comes to life. This is the one time a week where they get to see the child shine—not just shine in her own right, but soar above her peers in extraordinary ways. Many autistic clients have superb abilities that Dr. Treffert calls *genetic memory*. Clients who have never been exposed to instruments before can improvise and play any instrument placed before them. They also crave to play anything they just heard, and express tremendous emotion through the fluidity of their spontaneous compositions. This is nothing short of a musical gift, one that deserves to be nurtured.

Music therapists are trained to find an area that needs work and then incorporate music into the session as a tool for meeting goals. Some use the term "adaptive piano lessons" freely when giving instrumental instruction to a special-needs client. This is an incorrect term, because music therapists are trained to adapt the material to the student's learning style. Instead, the piano teacher should adapt her teaching style to the material as needed.

Students who first experience adaptive piano lessons may walk away playing but possess few skills transferable to the real world. Many such students are even taught with color charts, shape symbols, letters on keys, or cheat sheets rather than being taught traditional sight-reading and technique. Colors do not relate to music at all, since using the letter names builds up to the next level of instruction. In adaptive piano lessons, theory instruction may fall to the wayside as the adaptive lesson focuses on end production rather than on the process of independent accomplishments throughout the student's musical study. The student learns to master a repertoire, but might not be able to converse with other musicians in the acceptable lingo. In turn, if a musically gifted student hears colossal works in his or her head, he or she might be hindered by his or her inability to write down his or her compositions. Finally, if Jimmy joins the school band, he will not be given the music with colors, post-it notes, and animal stickers on it.

In the Rancer Method, everything is taught as a steppingstone to sophisticated material. Music theory helps the student begin to understand the abstract concepts necessary for higher learning in academia. Understanding of theory reinforces the note reading from a conceptual perspective, a skill unavailable at first to many special-needs students. Theory is a major reinforcer for reading music and is woven into the lessons through the Rancer Method's technique in a way that's painless and fun. The music books used in the Rancer Method are bought in a music store, a "normal" thing to do, so this is when parents realize that this is a "normal" activity, vastly different from the heavily accommodated activities their child is involved in each day. Often, siblings will ask that they too be taught, since their brother is having much more fun than they are at their music instruction elsewhere.

First Steps

The most important thing when starting a student on piano is to introduce him to the letter names versus the notes. The letter names are presented in positions C and G, first starting with the right hand and then eventually adding in the left. The reason this is so important is that when a child opens the book for the first time, he automatically understands the letters and has no opportunity to say, "I can't do it" or "I don't understand." Once he is shown which finger goes on which key for each letter, he automatically gets it and starts playing. Neurologically, associating the letters on the ascent makes it a smooth transition for kids to match their fingers to the letters on the descent. This begins the bridging of motor association regardless of cognitive level. It is important not to label the keys with stickers or labels of any kind, since it disrupts the associations that need to be mentally computed.

1. The Slide (4/4)

C D E F | G G G – | G F E D | C C C – ‖
Climb-ing up the   play- ground slide,   Down we glide a   speed - y ride.

2. Tower of Blocks (3/4)

C–D | E–F | G–G | G– – | G–F | E–D | C–C | C– – ‖
Build - ing   up   a   tow'r of blocks,   Down it   flops if some - one knocks.

Reprinted with permission

After finishing both books 1 and 2 of the *Keyboard Talent Hunt* (Schaum Publications), they can now transition into reading notes (the *Alfred* series). The letter names are merely the "cake" to which the notes add the "icing." Some students begin lessons after having already been introduced to note reading by family members or teachers. Nonetheless, those students are re-taught with letter names first, to give them a solid foundation that carries into note reading. As they fly through these books regardless of their previous experience, their self-esteem soars since they feel so smart.

The music in the book is not all children-oriented, so even adult learners benefit from this system, as witnessed with a sixty-year-old client with dementia. When starting, adults are still introduced to children's books. They're told that the learning style is the same, and that it's preferable that they fly through the children's books rather than being so stifled by the adult books that they then quit.

A student with absolute pitch might be playing at an advanced level but will enter your studio with very sloppy fingering. The fingering in both of these methods is inherent in these books (*Keyboard Talent Hunt* and *Alfred*). The Rancer Method focuses on perfecting fingering before note reading is introduced.

Case Studies: Physical Challenges

Case Study 1: K is a ten-year-old autistic client who entered Susan's practice a few months ago after bombing out with three other teachers in the past two years. He walked in obsessed with theory and blues improvisation, turning every film score he heard into a blues tune. Out of extreme boredom, he challenged himself to transpose them into other keys, using theory to guide him. Yet with all these abilities he couldn't sight-read well enough to produce on the same level as his other skills. He first came with very poor fingering, using only the same four fingers (middle and index from both hands). Though his motor skills were poorly developed, the music drove him to follow the methodology in the *Alfred Basic Piano Library*, and his fingering is improving dramatically each week. He continues to fly through the method books, practice on his own, and love playing. When his grandmother observed him at a lesson, she complimented Susan, saying, "You've made him into a different child."

Case Study 2: Sid is a non-speaking autistic student who also has Down syndrome. His joints hyperextend, and his fingers are floppy and sink into the piano keys. Regardless of the motor skills needing extra time to catch up, Henny pushed him intellectually to motivate him to stay engaged in the learning rather than focusing on his finger frustrations. Henny relied on his savant math skills to presume competence, and Sid reciprocated by rising to every new challenge. It became increasingly important not to dwell on anything 'babyish' or Sid would refuse to engage in the lesson or practice for that song. When he transitioned into note-reading, he had to be taught the more complicated chord before the basic technique just to keep him interested. Sid has a photographic memory and is moving into level 2 of note-reading after one year of lessons. When his mother surveyed him on Henny's teaching, he scored a 10 for everything except his enjoyment during the lesson. Sid is a social child who prefers to make music with others and is finding the private lessons to be isolating. We remedied that by recommending that he practice publicly, perhaps in a nursing home or at a local community room.

Case Study 3: Samuel started working with Susan at age three. His ear was very dominant, but he had no finger control. Due to his autism he had poor motor planning and poor executive function. His skills were very disorganized. Sam would get very angry when he was instructed to correct anything. Any pointers from Susan would trigger a major meltdown. Now in the seventh grade in a private school, Sam is thriving. He's able to recognize when he needs a break, and requests it. This way, he is able to regulate himself. His fingering is now impeccable, his playing is smooth and confident, and he soars. His sight-reading has improved, and his speed has increased so he can feel comfortable reading as a tool rather than a hindrance. Sam now appreciates what he can do; he is in level 5, and can compare himself to his peers. He is devoted to improvising, a classic need of an absolute pitcher to feed the insatiable appetite for sound.

Sam always had trouble deciphering the notes. Even today he struggles to answer, "What note is that?" Also, he couldn't recite the alphabet backwards, such as on a descending scale. Susan had to write the letters backwards on the page so he could memorize the sequence of what they sound like rather than calculate them in reverse. By giving him this information, you, the teacher, are saying, "It's okay," rather than torturing him and making him feel stupid. Eventually he learned it and is now doing fine. When preparing for his Bar-Mitzvah, Sam will have no problem remembering the melody of his Torah reading—that's the bonus of his gift. At his Bar-Mitzvah service, he will be performing an improvisational piece that strikes him at that moment.

Free Time

After the student plays her assigned piano pieces and a new assignment is reviewed, the rest of the session is devoted to free time. This is seen as a reward, motivating the client to make choices in a format where he or she can express herself through music, which is so easily accessible to him or her. With so many forms of expression, music is his or her highest demonstration of communication that her parents witness in contrast to everywhere else.

The musical gift provides individuals with the language for bridging the gap between his world and the world around him. By empowering him with the gift of music education, the individual can now learn the meaning of those dots on the page, just like the professionals do. Suddenly, he has the vocabulary to read and write his own music—a star is born!

Introducing formal sight-reading for piano strips away the ear and strengthens the visual processing because the client is now compelled to refer to the notes in order to produce intelligent music. This develops better reading comprehension, which helps to fulfill academic necessity. Forcing oneself to develop visual processing through sight-reading music strengthens the skill set while providing the most satisfactory sound to act as a very rewarding reinforcer for AP possessors who crave sound at all times.

In the field of music therapy, clients who meet their goals are discharged instead of being transitioned into studying an instrument. Realistically, music therapists are most qualified to start the client on learning an instrument. The piano is preferable because of its linear design. To maintain students as therapy clients is important since their journey has just begun.

A typical music therapy session is structured around a prepared session plan, as taught in the university curriculum. The therapist will play/perform, and gently offer the client the opportunity to accompany on a drum or instrument that doesn't require formal instruction. This is what Susan considers a free-time activity, one not calculated to contribute to educational value and the client's well-being. When used as a reinforcer, however, the free time becomes an opportunity to see clients apply themselves, giving their all to piano study at the start of the session. Offering them the dignity of formal instruction builds their self-esteem, as they see themselves in a "normal" activity, whereas everywhere else in their lives they are consumed with special education and therapies designed to minimize adverse behaviors. For once in their week, they can spend time expressing an ability rather than being controlled to suppress a behavior.

Parents constantly report that this is the one place their child has fun. They also report that in the other therapies such as speech and occupational therapy (OT), they are constantly being told what their child cannot do, while in the sessions they are shown what their child *could* do. This has also become the beginning of building a bridge between the child and the community, as these students, with their newfound abilities, can now be integrated into summer music camps, local church choirs, etc.

Case Studies: Self-Esteem and Cognition

Case Study 1: B is a shy sixteen-year-old boy who has been coming to Susan since he was four. B has some learning disabilities, retinal damage, and other medical issues. He first began with piano, and then added guitar. In school band, he decided to take up clarinet. Susan was concerned that it was a Bb instrument, and with his absolute pitch, he would have to transpose, but B did just fine with it. Because of his shy nature, Susan had to instruct him to tell his teacher that he has absolute pitch. Once the teacher figured it out, she had him tune the band, and now lets him answer specific questions that have to do with pitch. She knows his abilities, and this empowers him in the class. He feels very special—like Susan told him he would.

Case Study 2: N is a seven-year-old autistic boy, and is functionally nonverbal. In his first session with Henny, his frustration with communication made him beat his head with his fist while crying. After many breakthroughs, week after week, everyone—including his school counselor—has reported back on his increased vocalizations and communication skills. N has perfect pitch, and would've fallen into the trap of feeding his ear with sound had he not been introduced to fingering and technique prior to note reading. Teaching note reading first would have slowed his production of sound through the piano, which N relies on to make his needs known. On one particularly snowy day, he played back an assigned song, but in minor key. He wanted to make sure everyone knew that he was feeling very dark at that moment. With his extraordinary progress, N's mom intends to mainstream him for the next school year.

Case Study 3: L is a twelve-year-old autistic girl who struggles greatly to regulate her intensity. She speaks in a very loud volume, and when she writes, she often breaks the pencil lead. Because she has been coming to Susan since she was three, L's piano playing is smoother now. In their sessions, Susan recently began focusing on dynamics. In her daily life, L is constantly humiliated when teachers and therapists tell her that her voice is too loud. "Why do they always tell me that?" she cries. For the first time in her life, however, being told how to regulate is okay, because it occurs in the context of music, and the composer is telling her how to do it, making it "correct" for that piece. It's not personal or directed at her supposed flaws. L is doing very well, regulating her singing and piano playing. Until she learns to feel the sensation of her own dynamics inside her body, L uses the simple tools she's been given to self-regulate. By placing two fingers on her throat, she can feel the difference in volume from the outside. With absolute pitch, L has the extra sensitivity to take clues from such small stimuli. This is an example of using an ability as an asset for developing self-perfection.

Case Study 4: B is a ten-year-old autistic boy. He comes from a long line of musicians. Recognizing his abilities, photographic memory, and very strong AP, Susan was able to show B what he could do. He resisted working on theory, but when Susan showed him that he could, he took the lead and began to learn it with zeal. Susan offered to let him choose his weekly workload so he could gain control over his progress. From there, he took off at a rapid pace through the books. He is doing terrifically, and his musician parents are thrilled for him and delighted that the family tradition can continue.

Sight-Reading and Piano Notation

Students with extreme right-brained visual processing challenges struggle to track lyrics on a page while also reading the melody line to sight-sing. As the lessons progress, their field of vision expands, and that difficulty becomes a thing of the past. In every area of life, tasks that rely on eye tracking will dramatically improve.

Some autistic students might also have a diagnosis of hyperlexia, which is an inexplicable and unusual ability to read at a very young age—between one and two. Often, hyperlexia can be an indicator that splinter skills may also emerge, which is typical in savants. For hyperlexic students, comprehension is often secondary to their sensorimotor response to printed symbols. They commonly struggle with sight-reading because they get hung up on reading the words and notes. This is too much information, and there's no room left for correlating it with the fingers and the sound. During free time, hyperlexic students will visually track the words on the page and lastly, glance at the pictures.

During improvisation, such students will benefit from picture books in which there are no words. While the student is sight-reading in a lesson, the teacher should cover up the lyrics, title, and directions so he or she doesn't see it. Some students might need to be able to read it just once and be done with it; then they can move on to the sight-reading. Letters and numbers are a compulsion for hyperlexic learners, who can't *not* read it. For such individuals, books can be used as a reward during mealtime. A system that worked for one individual was "One bite, one page."

Hyperlexia can also indicate that the student is a "left-brainer" and likely has a photographic memory, which is often permanent in nature. Such students struggle in the first series of instruction with the *Keyboard Talent Hunt* books. This becomes even more prevalent in the second book, when playing with both hands simultaneously. As they move through the lessons, however, these students flourish in the note-reading books. This is because a person with a photographic memory has an instant snapshot of the page stored in his memory. This snapshot stores the mathematical intervallic relationships computed by location of the notes. Such students should be directed to practice only once a week if they get bored too quickly. To them, it feels like rote learning and mere reproduction of the image in their heads, but it greatly benefits the development of their motor skills if they can be encouraged to practice twice a week.

When they have to read musical letters on a page, rather than notation, hyperlexic visual learners struggle to make sense of it. This is because the letters aren't words and it's therefore difficult to sequence them into logical patterns. Rather, the student has to mentally translate those letters before playing, which can be cumbersome. This is a mental process similar to reading in a different language and understanding the meaning of the sentence only after translating it in your head one word at a time. A high percentage of such students display signs of photographic memory. More important, these are the students who will become very proficient sight-readers and make excellent candidates for music study in college.

When introducing notation, it's important to provide eye-tracking clues to develop the visual processing. By marking the G line of the treble clef staff and the F line of the bass clef, the student can refer to it when she gets lost visually. These lines are used as focal points. In time, the eye is able to track a line continuously, and then slowly develop to see the areas above and below it. Some students must have those lines highlighted in bold colors, or they cannot distinguish the *fore* from the *ground*.

When the student progresses to the bottom line of the bass clef, we then call the bottom line the G line and measure from that. There's a reason why the treble clef is called the G clef and the bass clef the F clef. Use that in your lesson, rather than altering the intentional designations. Refrain from incorporating mnemonics such as F-A-C-E or Every-Good-Boy-Does-Fine. These associations defeat the purpose of eye tracking in note-reading exercises.

Suzuki is an example of a system that produces a performer in no time who values the product. Suzuki starts off as a total auditory program. Students with absolute pitch will excel, as they can play anything back effortlessly. Most piano teachers will bemoan how difficult it is to teach a former Suzuki student to sight-read. The process becomes grueling and the student might very well quit. Therefore it's crucial to teach only once and teach correctly, with the greatest benefit to the student.

A child who's learning violin by the Suzuki method will learn how to hold the instrument and learn how to bow it properly. Everything will be so easy for her that it will look like she's a fabulous player. Later, however, when she learns to note-read, such struggles emerge that she might end up quitting music forever. This can be avoided by assessing the learner's style early in the teaching process. When students eventually get to college, they must be able to sight-read proficiently at auditions in order to be accepted into a music program; if unable to, they won't be accepted.

Important Do's and Don'ts

1. **Fingering** – RBAPs struggle to assign abstract values such as numbers to something tangible such as fingers. When teaching, never say, "Use finger number three on the E." Instead, correct fingering by saying, "use your C finger" or "oops, fix your D finger" or touch the correct finger.
2. **Metronome** – Even the most sophisticated gadgets produce a pitch. For the finely tuned individual, this sound causes great interference while trying to produce on an instrument. The competing tones will set the student back when practicing to refine her technique. It can be used when she has reached a more advanced, more disciplined level. You can't just turn it on and assume that the student will just pick up on it. A metronome might have very short-lived utility. Though it has been successfully used with upper-level students, they all profess that it was a very painful rite of passage. Working in an ensemble is the best way for aural learners to pace themselves. To force it during practice is too grueling and intense when the tones compete with the individual's personal focus on her own sound. With the competing sounds, it's like carrying on two conversations simultaneously.
3. **Behavior** – Autistic students will stim when they're anxious, overwhelmed, or excited. Forcing them to stop stimming (self regulatory behaviors, e.g. hand flapping) is cruel, so please

get over any discomfort you might feel with such behaviors. If the student must look away from his fingers to be able to recall the sound, please recognize that the visual is interfering with the auditory. Forcing a modification of that behavior will detract from the ear.

4. **Posture** – If the student rocks the piano bench, understand this as a sign of frustration at the sound not coming out of the instrument fast enough, because in his or her head he or she hears it as a whole. The level of annoyance can be very high.

   A students might also use the pedal in strange ways, such as leaning his or her foot at an angle off the pedal, or with his foot half in and half out of his or her shoe, or even barefoot. This is so he or she can produce the sound as fast as he hears it. Using certain postural changes helps keep the flow untainted, thus manipulating the sound to come out faster.

   A student might stim on the pedal. Do not make it an issue and force her to stop clamping down as she's thinking through the notes. Rather, allow the use of the pedal as a reward for more fully trained students who can analyze the theory of the chords in the measures. Label them with roman numerals, and encourage the individual to use the pedal until the next chord change. In Baroque music, she'll stop using the pedal when she realizes how complex the chord changes are, and also hears how gross it sounds, since it messes with the melody line. Otherwise, let it go until she develops the sophistication to understand it independently.

5. **Vision** – Students with severe RBAP struggle to see the music. They might lean in with their noses straight into the music. When they say they can't figure it out, they're not trying to slack off or look for excuses. They're operating on empty and yet are still producing. In some cases, the area they can visually process is no bigger than a pencil eraser. Therefore they certainly can't see both clefs simultaneously, and also can't see chords that stack multiple notes.

Some students might report the staff lines as wavy or jumping around. Others might not be able to see half notes because the thin outline interferes with the staff lines. Whole notes usually have a thicker outline, making them easier to distinguish. It might help to highlight or fill in the half notes with a color, to make it stand out from the staff lines. Most RBAPs read music better if there are no staff lines, so if the lines must be there, they should not dominate. A pale-yellow page with gray staff lines and black noteheads are best. On the iPad, the screen contrast should be adjusted. On printed music, colored no-glare filters should be placed over the pages to reduce contrast.

6. **Rushing** – the student rushes through a piece every single time, with no perception of his speed. If forced to slow down, he has trouble doing so. Some complain that it no longer seems like it's the same song, or that they don't know where they are in the song anymore. Please respect that they truly cannot slow down. The skill to play it comes from a perfect reproduction, and altering that perception isn't possible. To produce it in another manner requires the ability to rotate the sound in one's head—a skill that leans away from extreme right-brain abilities.

7. **Practicing** – Students with AP/RP have major issues with practicing over and over again. When the melody is permanently stored in auditory memory, playing it repeatedly might cause the student to memorize wrong notes, as the reproduction would not be accurate each time it's played. Such students also struggle to play something when corrected once they've heard an incorrect recording. Undoing the damage of storing it incorrectly is a lengthy and painful process that can be nearly impossible for the severely right-brained. With many years of work on sight-reading, the ability to create a new sound in one's memory strengthens, as eye-tracking exercises are directly related to that ability. If one can track larger areas on the paper, one can expand the ability to think abstractly. Such a skill allows

someone to create imagery symbolic of a sound heard, and rotate that image for advanced sequencing.

8. **Scales** – Never force the practice of scales, which are needed to help LBAP students conclude formulas rapidly. RBAPs think in pitch, not in accidentals or key signatures. They can produce a scale with the correct accidentals merely by listening, as they can feel it before they can speak it. They do not calculate or think it.

9. **Prompting** - Students will become adept at reading your nonverbal clues to guess the next note on the page. They can see your eyebrows go up to indicate that the note goes up. They notice your breathing to indicate the start of a new phrase. These are subconscious ways that we embody the material and therefore inadvertently give it away. To prompt the absolute pitch student, encourage the visual guestimation to stretch from piecemeal thinking to greater concepts.

In the transition to note-reading with the *My Piano Book A* book, just say "all of these are C's, even the empty one. When you get to the empty one, just do C-Hold". This prompt eliminates the panic of seeing notes and not knowing what to do. Since the student already knows C-position, and knows which finger to use, and also knows what to do for a 'hold', they usually fly through this with glee. When arriving to the last two pages, (p.24 and p.25), your prompts should be, "Sometimes we have next door neighbor notes, but sometimes we are skipping. In this song, we start on the? C, good! But then we skip, and finally, we go all the way to the G-line. Go ahead and try this song. Make sure you count your skips and your neighbors." If the student plays notes in the order, simply prompt, "Oops, make sure you count your skips."

Henny's student once said "the C is the lady with the eyelashes." Henny likes to think of the C as the one with the hands flapping. Another trick that works is to tell the student, "The D is right under the lines. Help! I'm drowning! Somebody please put me back in the lines!" The treble clef is easily made memorable with the right prompts.

In the *Alfred* series, rather than saying, "If this is a G, then what is this," say, "Here is your G-line. Next note is going up or down?" Student might say "up". Say, "Good. Seconds or thirds?" By the time the *Alfred* series moves into 4ths and 5ths, the concept of intervallic thinking will be cemented. I often explain this to the students with the metaphor of the lunch special: Imagine you are working at an office and you need to go to the restaurant to get the lunch orders for ten people. When you get to the store, you can say, "I need one fries, one fries, one fries, one fries, one coke, one coke, one pepsi, one coke ..." or, you can say "I'll have 4 lunch specials." Consolidating makes you more efficient in the workplace, and mapping out your intervals makes you a faster sight-reader. Once we move away from the Keyboard Talent Hunt book, we need to move away from the "okay, here's a G, and here's a D" mentality, and move into "Okay, here's a fifth". Students who follow this method ease into it with grace and power through the note-reading with tremendous joy. Continue to highlight the F and G lines until the end of the 1A books.

Autistic Students

> *Thank-you to Susan Rancer for teaching Daniel to tolerate notes and appreciate music.*
> —*Karen Crosby, California*

> *We were at the doctor's office for a checkup today. Listening to the doorbell, Oscar identified that it rings in a third. So I asked him, "what are the notes?" And he shot back: "G and E." I quickly tested on YouTube for a G tone—correct, of course!"*
>
> —*Peter Limbrick, San Francisco*

Autism is a genetically based human neurological variant. The complex set of interrelated characteristics that distinguish autistic neurology from non-autistic neurology is not yet fully understood, but current evidence indicates that the central distinction is that particularly high levels of synaptic connectivity and responsiveness characterize the autistic brain. This tends to make the autistic individual's subjective experience more intense and chaotic than that of non-autistic individuals. On both the sensorimotor and cognitive levels, the autistic mind tends to register more information, and the impact of each bit of information tends to be both stronger and less predictable. Autism produces distinctive, atypical ways of thinking, moving, interaction, and sensory and cognitive processing. Motor characteristics called stimming (repetitive motion such as hand flapping) and intense interests can be traced to those high levels of synaptic connectivity and responsiveness that are the key distinguishing features of autistic neurology.[8]

When you cross a music therapist who has absolute pitch with an untrained autistic AP individual, magic can happen. Susan and Henny can use their life experiences to separate the traits of the autism, absolute pitch, synesthesia, and sensory-integration issues. These blended experiences have helped instill dignity in many individuals who were previously misunderstood. Teaching to the gift reinforces positive abilities, and sensory behaviors begin to diminish.

Josie came to Susan when she was ten years old. Susan saw right away that she had a good ear because of her rhythm. On the piano, she never created anything, but she was very creative on the drums. Josie had a very hard time, though, learning to read the music, because she had dyslexia, Tourette's, anxiety, and major visual-processing issues. She was attending a one-to-one private school and was doing very well.

Reading rhythm and translating it to counting was a nightmare for Josie, but she improved a lot after working with her grandmother consistently. Despite Josie's dyslexia, she was able to learn how to read

---

[8] Walker, Nick. (2014) What is Autism? http://neurocosmopolitanism.com/what-is-autism

music just because she was first started with the *Keyboard Talent Hunt*. The book sets up all the skills for organization without requiring note reading. Once the student is solid in her technique, note reading is introduced in a non-threatening way.

For high school, Josie's parents wanted to move her into a more typical school setting to prepare her for college. When the family relocated, Josie was unable to continue with Susan. In a recent letter from Josie's family, the feedback on her successes is astounding. They wrote:

> Dear Susan,
>
> I have been remiss in not communicating before now, but know I have often thought of your contributions to Josie's life and planned on sending an email. Josie is doing well. Your suggestion of Sterne School bore fruit. It took them three days of auditioning before they admitted her, but she now attends Sterne and it's going very well.
>
> Josie has continued to awaken cognitively and socially. Of course there remain moments of frustration, but seeing her growth is like watching the sun peek through the clouds: it is visible more often as time goes by. Josie sees an excellent professional who gives her neurofeedback, and while I can understand that there are probably many quacks in this field, this is the real deal. It has been one of the important aspects of Josie's catching up.
>
> Josie trained in aikido for years. It is *wonderful* that she has supportive and wise teachers and role models. Aikido is a branch of martial arts that trains students to be aware and prepared. It is defensive, and though an effective tool for disarming an aggressor, is not

violent in nature or execution. I thought that many of your students' parents might appreciate this program. I recommend them highly.

Now for my expression of appreciation: Susan, thank you for working with Josie all those years; you were a tether to helping her growth and development as well as a significant mentor in her life. You really are the reason she is now at Sterne. Thank you for the stroke of inspiration that you offered as you helped me dissect our situation. Also, I feel deep appreciation for your support of me. When you find yourself in an ongoing day-to-day situation, it can be hard to find clarity. You and I had several significant conversations that strengthened my sense of what was correct, and helped reinforce finding a way out of the forest.

If ever I can be of any assistance, please don't hesitate to contact me. This journey has taught me much, and I'm happy to help others if I can. Thank you again for being one of the guideposts along our way. God bless you in your significant work with His children; may He watch over you and yours always. You have been and remain a blessing in our lives.

With fond appreciation,
Kathy

Learning Styles

The presence of relative pitch or absolute pitch is evidence of brain differences specific to auditory learners. The more prodigious the ear the more extreme the differences. Teaching the student with absolute pitch should not begin before an AP assessment is completed (previous chapter). The assessment is a fast, simple method for learning about your student before you design a course of study. Assessing for AP helps determine whether your student is an auditory, visual, or kinesthetic learner.

Caution: Students who have no introduction to music at all will be difficult to test. Give careful attention to such students when you teach them for the purpose of testing. The system of the Rancer Method specifically highlights when in the teaching steps a student should be assessed.

Auditory Learners

It's important to acknowledge that auditory learners will struggle to decipher the notes on the page. This is a visual processing problem, which also may involve a convergence disorder. A student with 20/20 vision will fatigue easily, as his or her brain stares desperately at the page, unable to distinguish the dot from the line. She might fidget or lean in close as she tries to find the best angle to read from. Her ear is constantly trying to hijack her eyes. This is a subconscious manifestation, sabotaging her visual learning.

This presents in a highly personalized level of extremity, which also correlates with the level of the ear. The more prodigious the ear, the more trouble the student will have with visual processing. Therefore, assessment of her AP variation is important, so you can understand what's happening right from the start.

- Visual learners must see information in order for them to form a mental image of an object or activity. Only then can they do well in exams such as multiple choice, since they can easily sequence the patterns of information and weed out the best answer.
- Auditory learners who tend to read aloud or mumble to themselves will reread exam questions numerous times, as they must create a mental image perception to derive meaning. To compensate, the individual reads aloud to redirect the information into another part of the brain, from the written word to the creation of a visual image or sound. As a result,

these individuals might have a mental image of the word spelled out, or have a fleeting kinesthetic reaction, either emotional or physical.

Once the translation of information occurs, you must give careful attention to how the person then recalls the information when tested. Has the information been processed and stored in the memory in the original way that it was first learned, or has it become stored in its translated method? Meaning, did they store it as a picture or a sound?

To be able to produce speech, a thought must travel from the memory, or perception of thought, past the emotion centers, and arrive in the left side of the brain, which is responsible for speech. In nonverbal individuals, however, the thought can still be typed, even if neural differences prevent it from connecting to the speech center. So too, careful scrutiny of how the person brings any information to the area of his production, be it speech, writing on a test, or performing at a recital, the pathways of how his or her data travels are going to determine how he or she will produce best on assessments.

- Right-brained pattern learners see many details as a complete whole pattern. They perceive a *gestalt*, but must process it for storage. Individuals who memorize facts using mnemonic devices are converting the *figure-ground* data set of details of the left brain into a *gestalt* whole for the right-brain memory. When the individual memorizes the facts by setting it to a tune, she is processing it as a *gestalt* whole, remaining in the right brain. Therefore right-brain recall will not occur if left-brain visual details are set before the student. A list of answers in a multiple-choice exam will not stimulate the right brain areas for the information stored as a *gestalt*. However, a who/what/when/where/why question is easy for the *gestalt* processor to answer, since the information is recalled as a whole. Such a student will be able to answer questions easily. The longer the paragraph requirement the better. Such a student will be able to write her way to the finish line no matter the assignment.

- For a music student who processes in the *gestalt* right-brain manner, performing at a recital will require him to play the entire piece. During practice, if the teacher asks him to play from one specific section, he might not be able to, since he has already stored it in his brain as a complete song. Separating right- and left-hand parts on the piano might be impossible at this point, after he has learned the whole song. So too, playing each part separately and then being asked to put it together might be impossible, since he has to hear it as a whole to store it and then play it as a whole. AP further drives this need, since the auditory memory of the *gestalt* might be instant, permanent, and highly accurate. Further, students with high levels of AP will reproduce by playing from the innermost recesses of their brains, including emotions, and might therefore deliver a very emotional, dynamic-rich performance. Such a student might "compose" to fill in the spots where he missed a note or two, in an effort to complete the full sound.
- Left-brained pattern learners see many details individually, and connect the dots to understand the whole concept. They extract the details from the data through *figure-ground* processes in the left brain, and only once the pattern is complete can they understand the bigger picture. These individuals rely on the written word to derive meaning, since putting each word together into a bigger pattern is how they learn. Such individuals do very well in math class where fundamental concepts are taught in incremental levels. They require foundational skills to be taught sequentially, until the greater concepts can be mastered. The right-brain learner might be able to master higher-level maths but struggle to compute algebra and earlier math concepts. These individuals memorize facts by recognizing intervallic patterns; they process the information as a figure-ground set of details in the left brain. Therefore left-brain recall will not occur if right-brain auditory or kinesthetic details are set before them. Such examples are oral class lectures, music recordings, and group and partner activities. Asking a who/what/when/where/why question is difficult for

these learners, since they don't know how many details of the complete pattern will answer the concept as a whole. Such a student will be able to fill in the blanks easily, since the missing word completes the pattern he has stored in his memory.

- For a music student who processes in the *figure-ground* left-brain manner, performing at a recital will be easy for him or her if he or she memorized the pattern. He or she will simply reproduce the pattern from memory, and do very well when playing Bach. He or she will easily continue playing after making a small mistake, whereas a right-brained student will first correct the mistake or return to a previous section. These stark differences in the reproduction depend on whether the song was stored as a visual pattern or as a whole *gestalt*. In the extreme left-brain processor, reproduction on his or her instrument might sound robotic and lacking emotion, since he or she might never have processed the pattern in the right brain areas for kinesthetic reaction, either emotional or physical.
- Kinesthetic right-brain auditory learners such as students with AP might have a fleeting kinesthetic reaction, either emotional or physical, when presented with information. This is heightened in individuals who have synesthesia, since they will also "see" the information in multi-sensory perceptions such as color, texture, taste, and emotion. Such a learner will often pace back and forth while deciphering meaning, and might also be a compulsive note-taker. He or she might never need to refer to his or her notes to understand or recall information, since the process of writing it down may be all he or she needs to process and store the information (Example: Writing a grocery list and not taking it along to the supermarket, since the memory is already stored after writing it). Such a learner will do best when pacing during an exam. Since that's impractical, one can accommodate this need by providing some basic creativity. The student can use fidget toys, squeeze a sensory ball, or sit on a swivel chair during coursework to best store and recall information. Such a student might not be able to count out blocks on the table,

but he or she can tell you how many blocks he or she is feeling if he or she doesn't look at them. Such a student can benefit when using fingers to count out math, by tapping on his or her lap. Sitting perfectly still and silent destroys his or her ability to recall information. Constant motion is necessary to stimulate the areas he or she needs to access. To create motion in a public place, such a learner might attach emotion to information as a means of learning. For example, "The sound of your name makes me feel tingly," or "The emperor of China was a brute." He or she will then recall the "tingly" or "brute," which will then remind him or her of the attached information. Therefore defining words on an exam is his or her strongest area.

- The music student who is a kinesthetic right-brain auditory learner might need to be shown how to play scales using hand-over-hand method. The teacher should not mention finger numbers or put fingering charts in front of the student, as these stimuli interrupt the need to feel the information. Such a student will prefer to memorize melodies through motor memory, and may spend hours practicing the same section over and over again until he or she can play it in his or her sleep. In fact, such students might not even need to be taught scales at all, he or since she can't make sense of their function and how it translates to theory.

These students do very well in vocabulary, and have a built-in thesaurus in their minds. Such a student will love how the *Apples and Bananas* song "feels" when his or her mouth contorts with each new verse, and might also be extra-skilled at making funny faces, dance, and language accents. They have precise control over how their muscles/tongues respond when there's a need to produce. Such a student might be able to accurately sing an "A" because he or she knows how and where to feel it inside his or her body. N, an eighteen-year-old girl with AP and progressive hearing loss, was able to sing a pitch on demand even though she could no longer hear it. Such a person becomes the choir member everyone relies on to stay on key, since she can hear the others but can barely hear herself.

What to expect when processing and assessment styles are not addressed:

- Auditory learners might struggle to sight-read music.
- Auditory learners might struggle in mathematics.
- Auditory learners might struggle with basic reading comprehension, often not realizing that visual-processing weakness is the reason.
- Auditory learners with 20/20 vision might struggle to visually process anything placed in front of them.
- An extreme auditory learner who has visual-processing challenges might peer at sheet music from the corner of his eye, or play around with his textbooks many times until he find a position in which he can see best. Such a learner might be overly sensitive to bright lights, as he can process better in dim lighting where there's less contrast between the ink and the page. Matte-colored plastic filter overlays can be effective in a brightly lit room.
- Extreme auditory learners might struggle with large-screen computers and TV's, and have a tendency to minimize screens into a small area. This is because the central vision is the only place where true processing occurs, and that area might be very small before treatment. Eye exercises prescribed by a neuro-ophthalmologist who specializes in perceptual disorders will expand this visual field dramatically. A teacher might offer large-print sheet music for such a learner, and then not understand why it doesn't seem to help him much. Rather, shrinking a page into an image on a cellphone screen might allow the student to see all the music, with one glance.
- Even in today's TV generation, eye-tracking observations of auditory learners reveal that they latch on to the sound to derive the meaning of the information they're watching. Auditory

learners might therefore struggle with charts or PowerPoint presentations if there's no sound.
- Visual learners might struggle to improvise, compose, or transpose by ear.
- Visual learners might ignore kinesthetic tools provided for computing, such as counting blocks for math tasks.
- A visual learner might struggle in ear training aural-skills studies, as he might be unable to envision a sound he just heard.
- Visual learners prefer to see the score to analyze the piece.
- Auditory learners prefer to hear the piece before analyzing the score.

A plethora of technologies exist to incorporate visual learning into classrooms worldwide, yet the auditory learner might often have to rely on audio textbooks and recording their lessons as the only way to stay on track within a program. Students with sensory integration problems often related to autism have very heightened auditory and visual memories, yet those senses don't integrate very well, which means that both systems will shut down when engaged simultaneously. This is where kinesthetic teaching is necessary.

Important Notes

- The extremity of a learning style is congruent with the extremity of the individual's ear on the AP Spectrum.
- A student with an ear that's very high on the AP Spectrum before teaching has begun is more likely to be an extreme auditory learner.
- After years of study, students may match the profile of a visual learner, even with the presence of AP. We call this a morph, when the individual begins to benefit from full-brain learning. This has been observed in the students who have studied under the Rancer Method for more than 30 percent of their lives.
- Visual learners exist with prodigious levels of AP, which is why the LB vs. RB assessment must also be used after assessing for AP.

Identifying your student's learning style is not enough. For the auditory learner, one picture is not worth a thousand words. We can't assume that the student is an auditory learner just because we assessed for learning style or because she matches that profile. How we learn is just the beginning of how information is organized. Temple Grandin started the process of explaining to the world how thinking in pictures works, but she describes herself as a highly visual learner, and has said only a little about how she thinks, which is separate from how she learns. Learning-style assessment tools are of little value unless they can be applied to teaching more effectively.

There are three parts to a successful educational relationship:

1. Learning Style – How the student learns information;
2. Processing Style – How the student thinks about the information; and
3. Assessment Style – How the student shows you what they know (i.e. exams).

Educators who use only learning-style assessment tools run the risk of pigeonholing students into processing and assessment styles based on their learning-style profiles. The Rancer Method is uniquely designed to capture the potential for educating students with AP who might have three different ways for learning, processing, and assessing. By observing extreme variations in the special-needs population, Susan Rancer has been able to formulate a system that works. Her program uses music books that are available in regular music shops, and organizes the books in an order that may be nontraditional to many classically trained teachers. Outside of teaching music, the Rancer Method can be adapted to any educational setting, since the method is adaptable for all types of learning. Though this book focuses primarily on teaching music, additional tips are offered for educators who choose to adapt this method to their educational settings.

Identifying the auditory learner is only the first of various clues needed for teaching. Researchers in the School of Education at

Johns Hopkins University have analyzed diverse assessment tools, including the Edmonds Learning Style Identification Exercise (ELSIE). In this test, upon hearing a given word, the person initially will either:

- Have a mental image of an object or activity;
- Have a mental image of the word spelled out;
- Receive meaning from the sound of the word without any visualization; or
- Have a fleeting kinesthetic reaction, either emotional or physical.

Why do some auditory learners think visually but can prove their knowledge only in a kinesthetic way?

Interpreting a student's learning style must also include the assessment of how he or she thinks and how he or she recalls information when expected to produce. For example, does the student in your class prefer answering essay questions or multiple choice? Does he or she do better in matching or short answers? Does fill-in the blanks confuse him or her? These are indications of the need for accommodating the way a student is assessed. Interpreting the styles for learning, processing, and assessment requires an overview of all areas.

Feedback and Frequently Asked Questions

Question from a piano teacher: Henny, what do you do with a mildly autistic student who seems normal except for distractibility and trouble controlling his emotions? He was able to move through printed material very quickly at first, but after a couple of years doesn't seem much different in his ability to learn the music. We've had our run-ins, but he wants to take piano. I had to remove him from group, and his parents came back a month later saying they wanted private lessons, which we're now doing.

Answer: Without observing him or knowing more, can you tell me how proficient he is at note reading? Can you identify precisely what trips him up? Perhaps he might be of the auditory RBAP subtype with a convergence insufficiency. If so, the fastest way to check is one of two things:

1. See if his mistakes happen more often on unfilled notes such as half notes and whole notes. People with convergence insufficiency can't tell where on the staff those notes are.
2. Watch his eyes intently while he's sight-reading something new. Is he doing the zigzag thing, going up to treble, down to bass, and back up again, note by note? Or is he floating above the soprano line and faking the left hand by ear?

Teacher: In the beginning he would make an effort to figure out all the notes and didn't seem to be faking anything, so he was able to play after a year what others were playing after three to four. He had also had some guitar. I don't know how much reading he was doing, but he seems to be able to recite the lines and spaces.

Henny: The notes might have been very close together, so he could guess his way. Do you play the piece for this student when you show him the music the first time?

Teacher: Yes.

Henny: Okay. *Never* play for him again. My vision is so impaired that when "reading" music, I fake it.

Question: For many on the spectrum, visual cues are processed more readily than verbal/auditory cues. How does your research and thinking account for that?

Answer: Photographic memory! Also, if there's interference, the stimulus will be processed in bits. With speech, if there are other sounds in the room, such as a fluorescent light buzzing, then not all the words in a sentence will be processed. With a photographic memory, however, one glance at the right moment, with no competing stimulus, is enough to retain the information.

Fran Young, Edmond, Oklahoma, November 2014
Piano teacher and author of *Improvisation on Christian Music*

> Too many teachers haven't a clue what to with the most extreme of these students. I have always been fascinated by the students who learn differently. I would say that most of my students have learning disabilities of some sort. I have been on a quest for years to learn more. The improv I've been teaching for seventeen years has given many of them a way of playing that has salvaged them. It is so rewarding to work with them and see them excel at this. Many would have never made it with a regular piano teacher.

Myra Brooks-Turner, Knoxville, Tenn.
Educator, award-winning composer, professional pianist, and freelance writer

> I have always enjoyed perfect pitch, and as a result still like to listen rather than look. When Ron (my husband of forty-three years) and I are in the car, he likes to have music as the background. To not hear it at full volume feels like having a bunch of little bees buzzing around my head. I'm not even able to think of other things and shut it out.

David E. Harris, Grand Island, Nebraska

> Thank you, thank you for your good article on perfect/relative pitch. It brought tears to my eyes because it so beautifully described traits I have lived with for over seventy years. All this time, I thought I was just plain weird and geeky! Understanding

oneself even just a little is truly one of the "Wow!" moments of life.

Question: Henny, please see this video of one of my autistic students. I'm having trouble fixing the stiffness and "beginner syndrome" of keeping one finger on the keys instead of all of them. How can we fix this?

Jordan Lane
Set Apart Studios, Littleton, Colorado

Answer: I see two important points. 1. This boy might have Ehlers-Danlos Syndrome; and 2. He's stimming on the keys.

Ehlers-Danlos syndrome (EDS) is a group of inherited disorders marked by extremely loose joints, hyperelastic skin that bruises easily, and easily damaged blood vessels. A geneticist must test for the hyper flexibility and mobility issues depicted in this image.

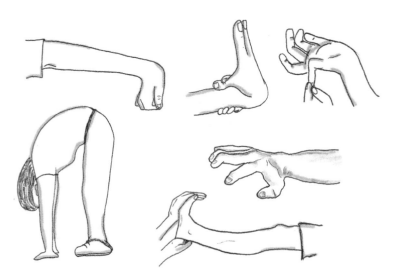

Hyper Flexibility and mobility issues in Ehlers-Danlos syndrome.

You might wish to offer the parents information and feedback within the scope of your professional practice. It's not your role to make a diagnosis.

Now for the stimming: He wouldn't do this if he were wearing gloves. I don't mean regular winter gloves or latex gloves, but specifically those ultra-thin cotton gloves that are worn as costumes (i.e. for magicians) or for overnight moisturizing treatment.

In order for him to process, translate, and produce so efficiently, he needs his brain to tie up three of the senses to work simultaneously. With sensory-integration issues, the autistic brain is going to love to work super-well, but only in isolation of the senses. In this case, to speed up his brain and get it all working, he needs to shut down the unneeded senses so he can power up the needed ones. The least-needed sense is touch. We need to respect his efforts at using his vision for sight-reading while also hearing what he's playing.

To silence his sensation of touch, he's giving it an overabundance of input via the stimming. This simple act overloads the tactile sense and makes it shut down. As a teacher, you can provide positive tactile input from other areas, leaving his fingertips free to play the keys without stimming on them.

My first suggestion is that you lower the bench and have him kneel by sitting on his legs—only when playing, not for practicing at home. This simple change in posture will apply force to his knees, which will take care of input from the waist down. In many kids, this is enough to shift all upper-body needs down and temporarily dissolve finger-stimming. You might also try the bathmat that I use, which I call the magic carpet (See my website www.HennyK.com/Resources page). He needs an immediate change in what he's taking in from other parts of his body, or he'll have to resort to gloves, which would shield his skin from feeling the ivories and rebounding from touch. Wearing gloves wouldn't offer the stim value of skin touch, so he wouldn't do it anymore; however, it's your responsibility to offer a new stim that can help him function at maximum capacity.

Question: My student (10) always says "that's difficult" every time the lesson is new. Yet, he transposes C major to C# major, F to F# major pieces and all the other keys he could come up with even when I don't ask for it. I benefit from it though because I have to transpose the teacher's part also. This is my first pupil who could transpose effortlessly. Why does he say that it's difficult if he can transpose easily?

Cleo Buenavista-Toribio, Philippines

Answer: Absolute pitchers can transpose without effort because they are mapping out the steps by ear. Over time, after years of training, they might incorporate some music theory in their transpositions. This student relies on his ear so much that he has not found a way to put it aside to decipher the notes on the page visually. Therefore, when he sees the notes, he hears it—and when he hears it, he can play it. His utterances of 'that's difficult' are a clue for you that he needs to learn that the notes are not a barrier but a tool for learning the piece. He would really benefit from the method in this book.

Question: I have a 16-year-old student who repeatedly closes his eyes when playing his song. His notes are incorrect, which is why it seems like he is playing a guessing game with his eyes closed. It almost seems like he's testing or trying to see where my boundaries are. He is unable to recall by playing a melody and will close his eyes when I ask him which notes he is playing. He is very intelligent and moderately high functioning. I sometimes have to prompt him four or five times to open his eyes.

Francesca Mackenzie, Abbotsford, BC, Canada

Answer: You describe a classic perfect pitcher who must recall from auditory memory, by recruiting the sound to emerge via touch. Such students will lose all recall when there is a visual disturbance. Your student might quite possibly have synesthesia in addition to absolute pitch. He needs to know where he is in space or he will get lost. His sense of touch is the most accurate for recall, which is why he is relying on feeling his way around to know how to best produce. Such students might also have particular difficulty with visual distortions such as depth perception, or counting notes on a staff line. To help him learn best, understand that he probably has a remarkable ability to feel out a I-IV-V7 harmonic progression in any key, so long as he can concentrate in the dark silence.

Question: Why does my student only walk on his tip toes? Also, why does my student place his hands on the keys and then push his hands/fingers back and forth between the front of the keys and the back, back and forth, back and forth before starting to play?

Liz Cunningham-Herman, Los Gatos, California

Answer: Many autistic people walk on tip-toes especially in the early years. It can be a tactile way of gaining feedback so they know where they are in space. When the Vestibular and Proprioceptive sensory system needs more advanced clues for balance, the clever trick is to put more force on the feet by shifting to the toes, so that more information is received with every step. Also, this student might be very sensitive to touch. The first touch to the keys is jarring because they are cold. By stimming on the keys, he is also warming up the keys so that he feels them with less shock. Once accustomed to the feel of the keys, he is good to go without recoiling over and over again.

Question: Why can't my autistic student keep a steady beat even though she reads notes quite well? Also, why can't she recognize and mentally group repeating patterns like broken chords in different octaves instead of reading notes individually?

Jessica Olson, Bozeman, Montana

Answer: Great question, Jessica. I would ask, "why doesn't she" rather than "why can't she." The rhythm might very well be a visual interference, where the student might not be able to hear what she is producing while reading. Have her shut her eyes and play a passage from memory, and her rhythm might be flawless. The method in the book is designed to get the perfect pitch student to make music with rhythm and harmony first. Once everything is coordinated, we bring in the notation. Students who need to be taught this way and are instead taught in the traditional theory-based method will find themselves picking apart note by note. To label the bigger picture, the student must first learn the bigger picture (gestalt) before the piecemeal. This is consistent with other approaches to gestalt learning. This student is a great example of where we don't want them to struggle and be turned away from note-reading forever.

Chapter Five

Music Therapy

Music Therapy is the clinical and evidence-based use of music interventions to accomplish individualized goals within a therapeutic relationship by a credentialed professional who has completed an approved music therapy program (*AMTA*, 2012).

Speech therapists teach the elements of speech, and occupational therapists teach the skills for functional tasks, so why shouldn't music therapists teach a musical instrument? Unless the therapist was not trained as a musician, she should consider the benefits for her clients when they're given the dignity of studying an instrument in the therapeutic environment. The clinical training for music therapists helps ensure that professional interactions will yield results through the therapeutic progress in the sessions—without the pressure of living up to a teacher/student arrangement. Every person has only one chance. If the teacher takes that chance away, the child becomes uninterested in pursuing music any further because he or she feels like a failure. This is worsened when it's the parent who wants the child to study the piano, thus pushing him or her into that arrangement with a teacher.

Music teachers adhere to the classical tradition they're trained in, but that tradition isn't necessarily practical for use in the studio.

A non-visual learner who's an out-of-the box thinker is seen as not conforming to the age-old discipline, and is therefore marginalized and punished for his or her creativity. At that point, his or her parents are considering a "special needs teacher," thinking that something's wrong with their child. As a result, students with AP who don't succeed are left with a demolished self-esteem. Music therapists are trained to incorporate techniques that promote sensory integration and positive reinforcement. They put themselves on the client's level rather than demand that the client put him or herself on the music teacher's level.

There are two popular options for musicians who go to college: Music Education or Applied Music, which is a degree earned for performance on the musician's chosen instrument. Because there are few jobs in these areas, many music majors end up teaching private piano lessons. Since they weren't trained to teach on this specific instrument, they teach according to how they were taught as children. The problem is that they weren't taught correctly in the first place. Many such individuals don't have absolute pitch, so when they get a student who is an auditory learner, they get frustrated with the student. The child isn't focusing, jumps off the piano bench, and exhibits a brief span of attention to what he or she's supposed to be learning.

Susan referred an AP individual to a specific piano teacher, knowing that they both had AP and would be an excellent fit. The student's mother told Susan that the teacher would always play the boy's piece for him right before a recital so he could perform at his best. *True story.*

Music educators are trained in the classical tradition to inspire discipline in their students' work. The student must fulfill the teacher's expectations each week. Some teachers require the child to audition to make sure he or she's good enough for the teacher's studio. This way, the teacher is assured that the child will perform well at the recital, so the teacher looks good. Learning an instrument is not about making the teacher look good; it's about teaching to the student's ability level, so that he or she can grow and develop mastery to his or her individual potential.

The standard in piano teaching involves meeting these goals:

1. Posture;
2. Practice;
3. Scales;
4. Note reading;
5. Technique; and
6. Recital.

The American Music Therapy Association publishes the standards of practice for music therapists as:

1. Assess development and needs;
2. Establish non-musical goals and objectives;
3. Plan sessions to meet the objectives;
4. Meet the goals; and
5. Discharge plan.

Susan adds musical goals in addition to piano instruction so that discharge from music therapy becomes irrelevant. The basis for this is an understanding that it wouldn't be in the client's best interest for a speech therapist to set non-speech goals for the therapy. Susan works up to the client's potential, and therefore implements piano instruction so that the client can interact at a trained level with his typical peers. He can also achieve mastery at a performance level, and even pursue a college education as a music major. By including piano instruction in the session, the therapist works up to the client's ability level rather than pathologizing areas in need of "fixing." The client has a basic human right for the therapist to look at what he or she does have, rather than at what he or she doesn't.

Singing
A poem by Leah Kligfeld

I like to sing good songs but not bad songs
I like to listen to music
Singing songs is like a smile in the sunshine
Like a laughing cloud
Dancing with headphones on
Singing with guitar and piano
I like to sing with music in D sharp
The sound of the D sharp makes me want to kiss Rachel's cheek
D sharp smells like making chocolate chip cookies
And looking at starry nights
F sharp sounds horrible to me
So do D, F, and G
Like a sad, crying baby
Those notes bother me and make me feel terrible
Then I can't get them out of my head
Until I sing in D sharp and I feel like sunshine
All over again.

Examples of Standard Music Therapy Goals
1. Cognitive Development
    a. Increased attention span
    b. Better orientation to the environment
2. Motor Development
    a. Increased physical coordination
    b. Improved dexterity and flexibility
    c. Increased gross and fine motor skills
    d. Better hand-eye coordination
    e. Better motor-planning skills
3. Perceptual Development:
    a. Better auditory-discrimination skills
    b. Increased auditory concepts

4. Social Development:
   a. Improved communication skills
   b. Improved group skills
5. Affective development
   a. Increased self-esteem and self-confidence
   b. Develop creative self-expression in music

Examples of Client-Specific Goals
1. Provide communication in the language of music.
2. Develop musical growth (improve elements of music: rhythm and motor activity, pitch, dynamic, interpretation, performance, etc.)
3. Allow for musical commitment, which demands reality, order, responses to all stimuli, therapist's directions, notation, etc.
4. Encourage behavioral responses from the simple (beating a drum) to the complex (playing a guitar, composing).
5. Foster ordering of behavior according to psychological response level, to help the client move from a less desirable to a more desirable psychological level (i.e., change mood from sad to happy; increase motivation from low to high desire to achieve).
6. Bring about creative self-expression in music.
7. Provide the opportunity for the enhancement of pride in self.
8. Provide for both negative and positive emotional expression through music.
9. Allow the freedom to choose a level of response whereby the client can participate comfortably in the full range of musical involvement.
10. Stimulate the individual to accomplish a series of personal goals, increasing the assumption of responsibility for self-directed behavior in musical progress.
11. Provide activities for reality orientation.
12. Increase verbal and nonverbal social interaction and communication.

13. Provide entertainment and recreation needed in the therapeutic environment.
14. Establish a trusting relationship with a music therapist on a one-to-one basis.

Upon the initial referral to the music therapist, the parent is asked the reason for the referral. The diagnosis and the child's needs, challenges, and gifts are discussed. Contact information such as address, phone number, email, and the child's date of birth are noted, as is the date of the first session scheduled. Sometimes a musical history can be obtained during the initial phone call. Not surprisingly, there's often a family history of musicians, since absolute pitch seems to skip a generation.

When you first meet with younger clients, their parents typically accompany them. Parents will often be unaware of what music therapy is about. It's the role of the therapist to educate with information that taps into the child's reachable potentials. This is easily accomplished during the initial meeting, where the child is having too much fun to notice that an assessment is being made. Parents often take delight that their child skips into the following sessions, engaged and ready to improvise and try anything. Often, the parents' response is tears, as they've never experienced their own child interacting on so many levels. The biggest compliment is the parents saying, "My child never has this much fun in any other therapy he goes to." Parents often ask, "Can I take pictures?" so they can share with family, friends, and their educational team.

In the initial session, singing a song from a picture book gives the child an opportunity to observe and get to know the music therapist. The book makes the song come alive, which offers a multidimensional presentation of the material. Once the therapist seems like a "pretty normal person," the child will then take a leap of faith. Some sing along right from the start. They can't help themselves—music does that to people.

At this point, the therapist should begin observing the child for clues on his or her learning style and needs. Is he or she hooked on the words in the picture book? Is he or she perhaps a visual learner? Does he or she keep perfect rhythm, or match your pitch with unusual skill? Does he or she cover his or her ears and wail? Does he or she follow directions? If so, a happy cooperative child should begin improvising on any instrument that piques his or her interest. Upon return, the child will readily fall into the sync of interacting musically. This is a good time to assess gross and fine motor skills, language, and following directions. A great activity for this assessment is "The Circle Game" (see page 14 in *Hap Palmer Favorites*). Fine motor skills begin to be worked on at the introduction of piano.

During the sessions, the parents, observing, might be inspired to offer more feedback. They'll freely offer an expanded family history and will tell you about their child's special interests and quirks. These are important to document, as those interests can be incorporated as motivators in the child's learning.

How to Incorporate the Goals of Music Therapy

1. Provide communication in the language of music. This humanistic approach offers the presumption of intelligence in all people. Relying on the individual's ability to communicate, we use music as a language to tap into that ability. We believe that everyone has a right to communicate and be understood. For many clients, music may be their only way to communicate. A professional must make that ability act as a bridge to the rest of the world. For example, teaching the client a song such as *Over the Rainbow* gives her client a tool. Then, if the client actually sings it somewhere else, others can recognize it. This offers the individual a way to connect.
2. Develop musical growth (improve elements of music: rhythm and motor activity, pitch, dynamics, interpretation, performance, etc). Teaching the client a song that he or she can play on the piano can help him or her show off to his or her peers. A client who explores various instruments expands

his or her musical vocabulary, giving her access to many other musical worlds of which she can be a valuable participant.
3. Allow for musical commitment, which demands reality, order, responses to all stimuli, therapist's directions, notation, etc. By playing the circle game, the client reacts in a timely and orderly way. Musical directions such as "Put one hand inside the circle" require the client to respond by performing that task quickly and consistently. In a musical context, motor planning and executive function issues begin to organize.
4. Encourage behavioral responses from the simple (beating a drum) to the complex (playing a guitar, composing). Teaching the client specific rhythms or strum patterns until he can actually play a song empowers him to compose music that he is motivated to write. This can't be achieved before simple directions are followed and then layered with additional levels of complexity.
5. Foster ordering of behavior according to psychological response level, to help the client move from a less desirable to more desirable psychological level (i.e., change of mood from sad to happy; change of motivation from low to a high desire to achieve). Often, clients come into the session overwhelmed from hours of remedial tutoring and other weekly therapies. All they hear from their clinicians and service providers is what they cannot do. When they learn an instrument, all of that changes. Suddenly, they can do something—and even better than their peers. The client's entire demeanor changes once she catches on to her abilities. Make those abilities known to your clients, and compliment them on their achievements.
6. Nurture creative self-expression in music. Just strumming on any kind of instrument can bring this about. Clients will often remark on songs and sounds and thus encourage a dialogue. Stories of bullying will sometimes emerge during or after a specific song. The most astounding sounds of musical expression come out of even the youngest children when they're given the proper tools in the proper environment.

7. Provide the opportunity for enhancement of pride in self. Musical expression builds self-esteem, whether the client is creating it from scratch or interacting through accompaniment on a simple instrument. When a sibling sits in on a session, the client will shine as he shows off what he does each week. Parents sometimes bring other therapists to observe how positive the sessions are and the degree of their child's engagement in music as opposed to other therapies.
8. Provide for both negative and positive emotional expression through music. Make it safe for the client to pound on the instrument if he or she needs to. All that emotion does come out, and eventually he or she will ease into playing in a more even-tempered way. Some clients channel their frustration by improvising loud obnoxious melodies, and will even explain to you the scenes that they are painting with their sounds. Even if the music is not your taste, (such as the soundtrack for *Monsters and Vampires*), acknowledge that your client is communicating through the instrument.
9. Allow the freedom to choose a level of response whereby the client can participate comfortably in the range of musical involvement. For some, ask only that they simply hold an instrument. Joint attention is very much a necessary first step. This is the time when most parents sit and observe, open mouthed in disbelief. They might grab their cell phones and snap photos or videos so that others familiar with the child can actually believe what's happening.
10. Stimulate the individual to accomplish a series of personal goals and thus increase the assumption of responsibility for self-directed behavior in musical progress. Sometimes the client's goal is to get through an entire song without her interest wandering. Others might disclose a deep desire to explore the cello. Don't be afraid to grow with the client, as you explore the instruments together. Never turn down a client's request because you can't play a given instrument; rather, find some resources online so you can explore it in

sessions together. The client doesn't need your virtuosic playing; she needs your musical aptitude.
11. Provide activities for reality orientation. Any of the *Hap Palmer Favorites* offers the client an opportunity to connect with the norms of her peers. Additionally, offer material that's age-appropriate or above, to challenge, stimulate, and inspire the client. The music therapy session might be the only time in the week when his or her abilities are tapped into.
12. Enhance verbal and nonverbal social interaction and communication. Getting the child to sing is a big step. Parents are often shocked the first time they see this happen. Parody, or making up words to songs is the beginning of lighting the creative fire. Get silly, be spontaneous, and let your good energy rub off on the client.
13. Provide entertainment and recreation needed in the therapeutic environment. Teaching the client an instrument allows him or her to entertain him or herself and others. Encourage the client to show off his or her skill when he or she volunteers at a local nursing home. At the senior home, everybody is his or her friend and is happy to see a fresh face. The validation is very conducive to development of self.
14. Establish a trusting one-to-one relationship between the client and music therapist. The child values this relationship, and trusts that he or she will be guided in the right direction. The parents feel the same way. For many clients, the music therapy studio is their safe haven and the only place they can be themselves.

Methodology

In music therapy, the therapist is trained to meet the client wherever the client is. The therapist's goal is to work with what the client has to offer, and to nurture that. Music educators use their studios to prep the student into the discipline, while music therapists service the client's goals from an IEP (Individualized Education Plan, written by the assessment team of the State Department of Education). Those goals are intended to strengthen the skills needed in the academic setting. The goals always addressed in teaching piano are hand-eye coordination, fine and gross motor control, motor-planning skills, visual tracking, and attention span. A music therapist is trained to use therapeutic methods and incorporate music to meet those nonmusical goals. Music teachers need their clients to achieve musical goals so the students can perform well at recitals and make the teacher look good. The end product is the focus on musical education, while in a music therapy relationship the process is what's given primary value.

Special Education

Often, the music therapy client will also be enrolled as a Special Education student. The music therapist needs to understand and acknowledge that autistic people often have very high intelligence, just like non-autistic people. When a student presents with multiple challenges, the school district often reassigns him or her into the Special Education classroom. Special Ed is a scaled-down version of a typical education, modified to be teachable in whichever way the student can best grasp the material his or her peers are learning.

Dr. Temple Grandin has lectured passionately about the great need for autistic children to be intellectually stimulated, to encourage individuals to come out of their caves of comfort and find a connection to the outside world. Locking highly intelligent children into Special Ed is like taking a geologist capable of analyzing the molecular structure of volcanoes and confining him to a sandbox. A bridge must be provided that allows individuals to explore high-level subjects they can excel in. Music instruction is just such a bridge.

In the classroom, the student can learn the course material together with her peers. While the class reviews it, the student can best benefit from one-on-one review using auditory methods. Classrooms are typically geared to the visual learner, inflicting an undue burden on the auditory learner whose attention then wanders. Such students desperately rely on the music therapist to help them learn skills that allow them to demonstrate their intelligence and talents to the school district. Once their piano proficiency has advanced to a sophisticated level, the school can begin to consider mainstreaming these individuals.

Anecdotes

Case Study 1: P is a seven-year-old boy in the first grade. He has a variety of visual and motor challenges related to brain damage. Many of his behaviors and difficulties resemble those of any other seven-year-old diagnosed with autism. After a consultation with Henny, P was removed from Special Education for critical subjects. He remained with his Special Ed peers for recreation times. One month into the school year, P's mom reported: "P is doing amazingly well in school this year. His teacher totally believes in inclusion. P started day 1 with a desk in the General Ed 2nd-grade class three doors down from his Special Ed class. He's in the Gen Ed class for math, science, and reading, plus lunch—all the things you recommended. We're so pleased that they put him there, and that he's doing so well." P has been studying piano with Susan for less than a year, and has benefited greatly.

Case Study 2: T is a ten-year-old autistic boy who is functionally nonverbal. He is enrolled in a Special Ed day class. When Henny observed him in the school, she noticed T picking his nose and squirming in his seat when the class was given a math worksheet. Henny asked the teacher, "Did you know that T is a calendar calculator savant?" The teacher was surprised to learn that, since he was struggling to understand how to engage T in the lessons and was unsure what the problem might be. It becomes really easy to label a behavior such as nose picking to be a part of the autism. In T's case, however, Henny suggested that the teacher hand him several worksheets of 10th-grade algebra. T zoomed through the answers, and naturally, no nose picking was necessary to compute them. The teacher later wrote a letter of reference for Henny in which he said, "During our debrief she was able to provide valuable and practical insight into the sensory experiences of my students in the educational setting. Together we were able to determine strategies that would promote academic success, given the unique sensory experiences of each student." In just two years of study with Susan, T's progress has exploded to high-school-level proficiency. It typically takes a student a full year to go through a method book; T has reached level five in two years. He's well on track to achieving exceptional mastery of the instrument and is enjoying its benefits. T is self-motivated because of how good his playing sounds.

Case Study 3: E is a fifteen-year-old autistic high school student. She's been in Special Ed her entire life. When Henny observed E in the classroom, the students were reviewing some basic algebraic functions. The teacher was speaking very slowly, as if the students were toddlers, and E kept shouting out the answers to the problems as soon as the teacher finished writing them. In an authoritarian tone of voice, the teacher said, "E, I need you to raise your hand." After the third time, a paraprofessional aide approached E with a bundle of laminated cards from which E had to choose her preferred time-out method. She chose to leave the room for five minutes to read her favorite book. No one ever took a moment to acknowledge that E was calculating algebra in her head, and instead of giving her academic accolades her behaviors were brought out to an ugly forefront. Henny encouraged E's parents to prep her to take the GED (high school equivalency) exam as soon as she turned sixteen. A student such as E would excel at a local community college, where she has the parental support to pursue her favorite subjects close to home. At age six, E briefly studied piano with Susan, but quit in pursuit of other creative interests such as horseback riding and painting.

Therapists Without Absolute Pitch

The music therapist doesn't need to have AP, but it's a tremendous asset so he or she can know how his or her clients experience sound. The observable clues for a client yielding to his or her ear and dismissing visual stimuli are decipherable only by one who does the same because of AP. The non-possessor is perfectly capable of teaching and guiding while nurturing the student's strengths—it's the awareness that's important.

Susan had a client who moved away for a few years. When she returned, her mom commented, "You know, we thought that all therapists could just sit down and play and sing any song, without the sheet music." The session is not about you; it's about the client. You need to be prepared for the most bizarre requests that come your way. Having absolute pitch gives you an edge, as you can focus on the individual in the session rather than on your performance as you reproduce from the written music.

A music therapist who doesn't have absolute pitch can still excel at the work. Your success will depend on how you use your strengths. Did you study oboe for four years and then get your music therapy degree? Well, let's turn that into a strength. First, recognize that you probably sight-read efficiently and can easily play any song the client demands, without having to hear it first. Unlike AP'ers, you can use sight-reading ability to your advantage.

It's important to refine your piano skills slowly but surely. You don't need to be the grand master to be able to teach. You don't need to be better than the client. It's not unusual for clients to master complex pieces later in their musical journey, pieces that you never attempted, but you need to be a step ahead of them in your experience. You must be able to understand every last dynamic printed, so you can guide your students to refine their technique.

Do not play their piano piece for them! You need to keep reminding yourself that classically trained teachers have a tendency to place a fresh new piece in front of the client and say, "Here's how it goes." That will completely destroy the process, impeding the client's progress. Remember, AP is a photographic memory for sound; therefore, the auditory learner will ignore the visual and just go ahead and play back for you what you played. You've triggered his or her auditory memory, and he or she now knows the sound of the piece, even if he can't play it back exactly at this time or at any time in the future.

Educate yourself – Be aware of your knowledge about absolute pitch. The stereotypes about AP'ers being a minority are inaccurate. The gift is no longer a phenomenon but is quite prevalent. Surprisingly, you'll find fewer instances among students and faculty at universities or music schools. To find AP'ers, go to drum circles or to free-improvisation groups. Music camps, weekends, and workshops catering to specific ethnic themes also seem to attract AP'ers, who seize upon any opportunity to make music without having to subscribe to the whole written code.

Do not sing or hum the melody. When you point to the music for the student, keep your voice in a monotone. Don't even breathe to the rhythm or tap the pencil in time. Your client needs to be able to decipher the sound of the written music. The tapping of your fingernails is the only clue that an astute AP'er needs. You might video record a few sessions with the camera focused on the client's eyes. When you later review the video privately, see what he or she does with his or her eyes. Every time she looks away from the sheet music, check to see what you did. It's often a sign that the AP'er received an auditory clue, and then focused on the instrument to reproduce the sound.

Free-Time Activities

This is the special time in the session that clients work hard to earn. Have a huge repertoire of music available to them. Keep a bookshelf handy, stocked with age-appropriate children's books with beautiful illustrations. Seek out books that have the story written in rhyme, so the words can be set to a familiar tune.

Make sure you're proficient in I-IV-V progressions in several keys. If your client cringes, you know he or she is not comfortable in that key, and you'll need to transpose. Most of the time free play will structure itself, with you playing guitar and the client accompanying on his or her instrument of choice. If you make it seem like it's normal to play any instrument on display, your client will take the dare and improvise as best he can. This way you can listen to his voice and watch his rhythm patterns, and begin to see traits of relative or absolute pitch.

Important: The client must be tested for his or her singing range to determine what key he or she is tuned to. This is important, so that you can match his or her range in musical activities.

When Susan's daughter, Emily, was twenty years old she visited France. Emily has AP, and immediately noticed that the people were speaking in a higher pitch than hers. She adjusted her French to match their pitch. Because of the authenticity in her tonality, people began to ask her if she was a native.

Every person is tuned to a specific key. For example, many Americans tend to be tuned to the key of C. Still, it's vital to understand that the client has a comfort key and a speaking key. Therefore she also has a standard key in which she will naturally sing. It's your responsibility to identify this key for each client. Your playing, singing, and accompaniment must be in the client's comfort key; otherwise, you place an extra strain on the individual to sing outside his or her range. Even if the client is not singing along, it can be uncomfortable or even painful (especially for autistic clients) to connect to a key that's above or below his or her inner tuning.

During the free time, be sure to slip in one activity of your choice so that you can monitor your client's' developmental levels. These activities focus on gross motor, following directions, right and left, and various milestones necessary for development. The parents enjoy watching their kids do these fun activities, while you get to see where they are developmentally. The children don't feel like they're being assessed, but rather feel musically supported to show off their accomplishments.

In the *Hap Palmer Favorites* book, introduce the songs in order of development, from early and simple to grade-school mathematics. The following activities are listed in this order:

1. Sammy, p. 48
2. The Circle, p. 12

3. Turn Around, p. 20
4. The Beanbag, p. 30
5. Listen and Do, p. 34
6. Triangle, Circle, and Square, p. 68
7. Knocking On My Door, p. 112
8. Put Your Hands Up In The Air, p. 8
9. Let's Dance, p. 10
10. The Circle Game, p. 14
11. Partners, p. 16
12. Touch, p. 17
13. Shake Something, p. 18
14. The Opposite, p. 42
15. Feelings, p. 50
16. Everybody Has Feelings, p. 58
17. All the Colors of the Rainbow, p. 66
18. Tap Out the Answer, p. 92
19. Building Bridges, p. 96

Picture books with exquisite and age-appropriate pictures with poems

1. Going To The Zoo, Tom Paxton
2. Raffi's Top 10 Songs To Read, Crown Publishers
3. Barney's Favorite Mother-Goose Rhymes, Volumes 1 & 2, Barney Publishing
4. Grandma's Feather Bed, John Denver, Dawn Publications,
5. The Marvelous Toy, Tom Paxton, Imagine
6. Over the Rainbow, Imagine
7. Puff the Magic Dragon, Imagine
8. On Top of Spaghetti, Scholastic Press
9. We All Sing With The Same Voice, Harper Collins Publishers
10. This Land is Your Land, Little, Brown Books for Young Readers
11. Itsy Bitsy Spider, Scholastic
12. Baby Beluga, Crown Publishers

For school-aged children

1. The Silly Billy Songs by Allan Katz contain parodies. A favorite is "Smelly Locker," published by Simon and Schuster.
2. There Was An Old Lady Who Swallowed a Trout, Henry Holt & Company, Inc.

Classic song books for children

1. The Disney Song, some pictures, mostly music with lyrics and chord symbols
2. Raffi Song Books contain the music with lyrics and chord symbols.
3. Sesame Song Books are a staple; pictures, mostly music with lyrics and chord symbols.

Manipulatives are activities that include the props mentioned in the song. The client is directed through the lyrics to add, remove, or select specific parts of the manipulative. For example, in the song *There Was An Old Lady Who Swallowed A Fly*, the client listens to the song as sung by the therapist. Then, when there's a pause in singing "She swallowed a spider to catch the ...?" the client sings "fly," then finds the little fly, and puts it into the stuffed grandma doll's mouth. These are available in *Old MacDonald*, and various other creative forms. Many of these songs come along with the manipulatives when purchased. Manipulatives might also be sold as Storytelling Activity Sets:

1. "There Was An Old Lady Who Swallowed A Fly" Doll, Music in Motion - Item 2267
2. Slippery Fish, Charlotte Diamond, from BubbleRock.com
3. The Pizza Song, *I Am A Pizza*, Charlotte Diamond, from BubbleRock.com
4. The Carrot Song, *Ten Crunchy Carrots*, Charlotte Diamond, from BubbleRock.com
5. "This Old Man" Doll by Music in Motion – Item

6. Alphabet Puzzle, for singing the *Alphabet Song*
7. Puppets with different facial expressions, for Hap Palmer's "Feelings," p. 50 and "Everybody Has Feelings," p. 58

Establishing Your Private Practice

When you work for a paycheck at an institution, your job is to meet the measurable goals. If your paperwork is correct, your services are billable and your job is justified, but in an environment like that, you confront the issue of sacrificing your own ideas for the sake of the funding. Even worse, there are music therapists who subcontract their work to newly certified students who are grateful for the opportunity for a steady income despite the steep cut their boss takes.

Having a home studio is the first step in establishing your private practice. It's not advisable to enter clients' homes, because you're invading their space and interrupting their activities. For the sake of transitioning, it's better for them to come to your professional studio, which affords them access to all the equipment and to opportunities they wouldn't have if you came to their door with a trunkful of musical instruments. It also gives a child with developmental issues the time needed to transition during the trip over to the studio.

Studio space in your home doesn't need to be large or lavishly outfitted. You need a comfortable spot for parents to sit. One or both parents should be present so they can watch the amazing progress their child is going to make during each session. (Most therapists ask the parents to leave.)

You should have a well-tuned piano and a quality keyboard with weighted keys, such as the Yamaha Clavinova—a sophisticated keyboard that has built-in song banks that, during free time, clients love to play by following the lights. This can improve visual tracking and fine motor skills. The static tuning is sometimes preferred for the more discriminatory ear of the very prodigious client. The weighted keys are necessary for the tactile input that the user needs to get the feedback as he or she plays.

Instruments – Your magic toolbox should consist of instruments such as hand drums, djembe, toca, tambourines, rainsticks, marimba, and assorted rhythm and percussion instruments which should be invitingly displayed on reachable shelves. In a closet, keep instruments in diverse sizes to suit children of various ages. Those should include guitar, violin, mandolin, ukulele, cello, accordion, tone bells, egg shakers, an autoharp, and a Qchord. You don't need to apply for a $6,000 grant to acquire these instruments—scout Craigslist and local flea markets. It's important that these instruments produce a quality sound and that they're real instruments, not toys. Mallets should be stored in a can with their heads up, so that students can help themselves. Always be careful to choose a mallet head that's softer than the instrument so the instrument doesn't get destroyed.

Piano – Align yourself with a local music store that sells pianos. Parents will want referrals to a place you trust. Have business cards handy, displayed in a corner area. You can get a referral fee from the piano dealer. Also, find a good piano tuner whom you trust. The tuner might give you a reduced fee in return for frequent service requests.

Books – Find a nearby music store and have them order the books that you'll use regularly. This way, you support a local business and they serve your clients. For children, the day they go to the store and buy their piano books will be quite memorable. You want to be a part of creating that memory. Your older clients will appreciate having access to the books they need so they can get started while highly motivated. They can also look at other books and start to dream of where they want to go with their music education.

Technology – Various forms of technology can play a major role in your practice. The iPad is useful for displaying lyrics for clients in a narrow-column, poem-like manner. The client can independently scroll while you accompany him or her. Apps such as OnSong can keep a scanned collection of lyrics sheets with chords all in one place, and chords can be easily transposed with the tap of a key. Your client might also enjoy improvising with the ThumbJam app. You'll need a speaker to amplify the sound, or a cable to plug into your Clavinova speakers. Many clients' favorite settings on ThumbJam are "Cello" and "Minor Key."

Footstool for the piano – Piano footstools are needed for younger clients to ground themselves without their legs dangling. Be aware that clients with developmental challenges will tend to kick the piano backboard. The Clavinova has models with recessed backboards, which provides instrument security for you.

Microphone for singing – A microphone on a stand is a great lure for some students who would otherwise not sing. The cable plugs into the Clavinova amp, and you have an instant instrument—just add a singer!

Furniture – Invest in a few small chairs for younger children to sit on during free play, and for any of their siblings who might sit in on sessions. The chairs should have no arms, so the clients can play instruments freely. Beanbags lack the support needed to keep clients engaged. When working with a group of children, seating them on individual carpet squares gives them a visual reminder of where their personal space is and where to stay put.

Lighting – The studio room should be well lit, but the light bulbs should be covered with fixtures. If you're designing a studio space from scratch, consider placing long bulbs behind the woodwork around the edges of the ceilings. It's important to have multiple light switches, allowing various lights to be turned off individually, so if a client isn't tolerating the light near the piano, the rest of the room behind her can still remain lit.

Marketing your Private Practice

Know and understand that you are entering an unknown world as business owner, financier, bookkeeper, marketer, and chief technology officer. This is your choice, and your college education might have not prepared you for any of it. Begin to learn from others' marketing strategies. For recent graduates, drumming up business the morning after graduation requires some mental calisthenics to use resources that are freely available. When you have no budget to invest, the Internet is your best friend. Your name will be your brand. To build your brand, you need to publicize a very strategic image. Learn from the strategies below:

Website – A professional website is crucial. Keep it simple. Set up the dot-com to be your full name. If you have a common name, and that name is unavailable for purchase as a dot-com, then add a word such as "studio" or an abbreviation for your state (e.g., "NY").

Telephone Number – you want a phone number that has a local/regional area code. This is important because people might search for a teacher near them by searching in their area code. For example, people in Manhattan might search Google for "piano teacher 212." You want to be that person who comes up on their search results. You want your phone number prominently displayed in the upper right-hand corner of every page on your website. You want it accessible, so searchers can sigh with relief, knowing they don't have to hunt through a maze of blog posts to find a CONTACT US page that leads them to a dummy submission form. When mothers decide to give their children lessons, they want a real-live human on the other end of the phone immediately.

Do not use your home phone number. If you can't yet afford a second line, use your cell number. Better yet, use one of the free online services such as Google Voice. You'll be given a free local phone number that forwards to your mobile phone or home phone. You can even set it up never to ring but only to transcribe voicemail as a text message to you or as an email. If you download the free app to your cell phone, you can return calls from the app, and the caller ID will show your Google Voice number.

Another reason to not use your home phone number is because people will google your number. You don't want your home address returned on Google search results, and it will be unless your number is private, which is hard to do with the phone company. Also, you don't want Aunt Marie visiting your family and answering your student cancellation calls while you're out buying groceries. Last but not least, when people Google your phone number, you want your website to show up, so make sure your phone number is entered as HTML text on your website's contact page as well as HTML text on your site header. Be sure that whoever designs your website doesn't add your phone number as a graphic onto your header design, as graphics aren't searchable by Google.

Internet Cleanup – Make a schedule to Google your name every month. It's important to monitor the web and maintain your image. If, two years ago, you "liked" a FaceBook recipe that happened to be on a public wall, then unlike it. No one needs to see your personal tastes in food or that you "liked" Target for a discount. When people Google you, they want to see your professional image. They want to see what kinds of articles you had published, so they can familiarize themselves with your philosophy and methodology. If you don't know how to clean up your name from specific sites, consult a geek friend who'll be happy to show you.

Check every month to make sure that Google has updated the archives and that you no longer appear in the cached search results. Also Google your phone number periodically, and make sure that the old Craigslist ad where you sold your end tables is deleted from search results. Clean up your FaceBook profile. You want all your information closed to public view and visible only to friends. You want your profile photo—which is open to the public—to be respectable and simple. You can create a public figure profile for yourself by adding "pages." That can become the page for your clients to "like," and that you update on professional information. Your FaceBook friends list should contain only people with whom you're friends, not people with whom you do business.

Getting Published – Offer to do a small write-up on the importance of piano lessons, and submit it to several local parenting magazines. Don't submit this to industry periodicals such as magazines for music teachers. Target the casual soccer mom who grabs a free copy of the monthly circulars available in supermarkets and doctors' offices. A bold headline of "Studies Show Piano Lessons Improve Math Scores" would grab parent's interest.

Scheduling – Be aware that after-school hours are the most desired, and you'll be changing your daily schedule to accommodate the stream of middle schoolers coming for lessons around dinnertime each day. Use the slack hours to schedule doctors' appointments, shop, and prepare meals. An important rule for new practitioners is to schedule your students on the same day, one lesson right after the next, so you always appear busy. This impresses upon parents that you have a full schedule, so they'll understand when you say, "Wednesday at 3:15 is the only time I have open." You want your students to see each other when one leaves and the next arrives. Parents like knowing that you have a thriving practice. Finally, lining up all your students on one day helps you focus and sustain momentum till the day is over. You'll cherish your memories of the time when you first began your practice—"Wow, my Wednesdays were so intense and so rewarding!" Never ask a parent, "What time is good for you?" Always suggest two openings, and let them choose.

Pricing – How you set your fees defines how your image will be built. Never settle for teaching more people for less money just because you're starting out. Increase your opinion of yourself; accept that you've studied your instrument for much of your life and have achieved a level of mastery that others want to pay to duplicate for themselves. Know that you are the deliverer of the path that needs to be taken. Stand tall and believe that you're worth more than $12/hour. Find out what the music teachers in your area are charging, and never charge as little as that. Then do a survey of the fees charged by local speech therapists, occupational therapists, and physical therapists. Your fee should sit comfortably among what experienced practitioners in your area charge for their expertise.

Do not charge the rate of a local math tutor; it undervalues your skill and reflects poorly on other practitioners. Uphold the dignity of your profession and don't undersell its worth. In the long run, you want to attract people who won't blink when they hear your fees, because they value what you deliver. That's the most desirable place to strive for; the alternative is working with underprivileged youth at a nonprofit where you're paid $10 per hour, if anything, and possibly from a grant that you yourself must write and submit annually for renewal.

Charging less at the start and increasing your price as you gain confidence is a poor idea and extremely unprofessional. Rather than raising prices every few months, increase your rates every four years to adjust for the cost of living in your region. Mail a letter to clients a few months ahead of time; for example, send a notice in July stating that you haven't raised your rates in four years and will raise them on October 1. Close by thanking them for their patronage. That's all.

The worst time to raise your fees is April, which is tax season. Also avoid raising rates in December, when people overextend their budgets to buy holiday gifts.

Population – Look around and make some decisions. Do you live in a remote village in the middle of nowhere? Do the people in your area generally rely on Social Services for survival? Do the local residents own or rent? Does the public school district have a music curriculum? Does the local Y offer free music lessons for underprivileged students? Are there support services for individuals with disabilities? Do they include music? Study the demographics and get to know the population you're targeting.

Patience – Accept that building a practice takes up to a year before you can feel secure that your steady client base will cover your expenses. Also understand the theories of marketing and return on investment. Typically, a parent will read your article or hold on to your business card and might stick it on the fridge for six months. One day, Johnny will come home from school angry and frustrated that he didn't get a part in the school talent show, and Mom will finally decide it's time to give him piano lessons. That's when you get an urgent call asking to be scheduled right away. You've been sitting and doubting yourself for months, wondering if you've made the dumbest choices of your life. When it rains it pours—the calls start to come in bursts, and suddenly, after months and months of silence, self-doubt, worry, and poverty, you find yourself with a waiting list.

Chapter Six

Our Fail-Proof Method

Transformative pedagogy must access open channels of communication for higher learning. The Rancer Method teaches to the gift of absolute pitch by augmenting musicality. When implemented correctly for 30% of the student's lifetime, the reading comprehension problems and struggles with mathematics will dissolve. Learning to note-read will be a permanent and positive experience.

Decoding and making sophisticated music releases adrenaline during the high-alpha learning state of the highly stimulating task, triggering neuroplastic changes in the visual motor cortex. In students with dyspraxia and motor planning challenges, the eye tracking improvement and independent finger movements will converge in the same time.

Piano Pedagogy: Structuring the Lesson

A lesson should be only thirty minutes long. Hour-long lessons are too lengthy for the student's attention span. You want them craving to come back, and if you satiate them, they might not want to, so time the tasks to fit into thirty minutes.

Begin the lesson with the student playing the material that was assigned to her at the previous lesson. When completed, offer your feedback in real time and/or afterward. Depending on the student's age, offer a sticker, stamps, or any of a variety of ways to mark completion of the assigned piece in the book. This is also a marker for you, the teacher, to see which assignments were completed.

Next, have your student play through the upcoming assignments so she'll know what to do in her practice time. This is the time for you to help her and explain new concepts. Write the date of today's lesson and the page number of the new assignments on the inside cover of the lesson book.

Lastly, your student worked hard and is now ready for free time, which lasts for however much time remains in the lesson. The importance of this component is outlined in greater detail later in the book.

Keyboard Talent Hunt Books 1 and 2

Begin the piano lesson with *Keyboard Talent Hunt* Book 1 (Schaum Publications). This book starts with letter names and puts the fingers to letters together from the start. The student is encouraged to keep his eyes on the book while feeling out the key using his fingers in C position or G position. The reward is the music he is making.

Do not label the piano keys with their letter names, because your student will learn from matching the letters on the page to the letters on the keyboard. Instead, they need to be able to perform mental calisthenics for the brain to figure which finger is in charge of which key. Be aware that the AP student will seek out sounds after seeing the music one time. This means that he memorizes instantaneously after playing it through just once. To recognize this, observe if he lowers his head, looks at you, or looks away from the music. Continue to point to the letters, encouraging the student to keep his head up and feel those keys to build motor skill and integrate his senses.

Remember: The AP student relies on auditory memory, often permanent in nature. When a student with absolute or relative pitch reads a simple song or plays a melodious piece of music for the first time, she involuntarily stores it in her auditory memory. The piece is captured much like a tape recording. Once this has occurred, the visual component of the piece can be removed and the student can play the same piece without reference to the notes. Ingraining the fingering as a motor skill is therefore critical in every moment of instruction so that a sensorimotor response occurs when seeing the notes. Pointing to the letters on the page is important—in the event that she drops her head, you need to be there for the student when she looks back up. Auditory learners such as those with AP are especially weak in visual processing and eye tracking. A student with visual-processing issues may be exceptionally prone to up/down eye movement when reading music and finding the piano key when she drops her head, so encouraging her to feel the keys without looking at them strengthens the visual processing.

The *Keyboard Talent Hunt* Book 1 is right hand letter reading for C position and then G position. After the student completes *Keyboard Talent Hunt* Book 1, go back to the beginning of the book. The same pages are replayed, using the left hand only, for C position in the first half of the book (up to song # 11). This is because your student has never seen left hand before or done anything with it. Finally, the motor ability to count out letters becomes a tactile operation rather than a hand-eye task, a fatal demand on the auditory learner. It is at this point that a very young AP student might be able to tell you that he heard "this finger" and hold up his index finger when he hears a D.

The student is then ready to go into *Keyboard Talent Hunt* Book 2, using both hands simultaneously. This book still uses letter-names, and ingrains the correct fingering for C position followed by G position. It is recommended that you highlight the right-hand notes in a color such as yellow so the student can distinguish the right-hand letters from the left-hand letters. Although unusual, it might take several lessons until the concept of left and right simultaneous playing begins to click. For those students, highlighting the left in one color and the right in another color seems to work. The parent might choose to mark a small dot with the highlighters onto the corresponding hands. Typically, only highlighting the right-hand notes in yellow is recommended.

After the completion of *Keyboard Talent Hunt* Book 2, the student is now ready to be introduced to notation. Note-reading skills are easily transferred from the previous lessons into *My Piano Book* A (Stewart, Glasscock & Glover, Belwin-Mills Publishing Corp, 1985). Only the first half of this book is used, through page 25. The second half is written in a position that shouldn't be used at this stage in the studies, because middle C and D in the right hand and middle C and B in the left hand *float* and are not anchored on the page (on the staff line). That disrupts the comprehension of the visual up/down of sound already associated to fingering.

This book now introduces the student to musical notes in a very slow reinforcing manner. (Teachers: You can lend this book to your students, since they usually work from the book for about a week). Having completed the first section of the book, the student now has learned to visually discriminate between step and skip notation in the right hand. The transition from letter names to note reading is painless at this point. Parents always react by saying, "I don't think my kid can do this," but are astonished when their children are playing like pros, their self-esteem through the roof. Now the parents begin to tell their friends and family that their child is studying piano, confident that he will continue to grow like his "normal" peers. It is suggested to some parents that they bring these books into IEP (individualized education plan) meetings. Since the staff at these meetings is often not musically trained, they're blown away that these "very disabled" children are able to do this.

My Piano Book A

First, go through the entire first half of the book (through page 25) and cross out or blot out all the letters printed as lyrics under the notes, so that the students have no reference. Begin your lesson by skipping straight to page 7. Always use traditional music terms rather than common language. Explain the following concepts:

- Treble Clef – Explain the treble clef, but mention that it is also referred to as the G clef (later explained). Show the relationship of the symbol—"When you see the treble clef, you play with your right hand."
- The Staff – Explain that there are five lines and four spaces, and that the notes are written on those five lines and four spaces. "Sometimes, notes are written above or below those lines. In this case, the C is written below the staff lines, on what's called a ledger line."
- Bar Lines – "Bar Lines divide the staff in the measures."
- Measures – "Measures are between the barlines and make up the musical sentences or phrase."
- Double Barline – "The double barline marks the end of your song."
- Rhythm – Explain the counting of beats. When pointing to a quarter note, say, "This gets one count," and demonstrate on piano. Then, point to the half note and say, "This note gets two counts," and demonstrate on piano. Do not play the song for him!
- The Notes – Talk about the notes: Start off with middle C. Say, "This is what C looks like in relation to the staff." Ask the student to place her hand on C position and go play. All of the technique from the previous two books kicks in. She's already learned the cake; now this is the icing. Watch her fly!

This method teaches one note at a time, and adds on till five notes (up to G) are all learned. The pictures are terrific and colorful, making it very inviting. The notes are printed in very large type, making it look easy, which is appropriate for beginners.

The G Line

Introduce the G line at around page 13, when teaching the letter E. Explain the G line as "the second line from the bottom, in the treble clef." The G line becomes the reference point for tracing the notes to the lines. With a pencil, extend the G line a bit outward to the left, and write the letter "G" above it. This is helpful for eye tracking and reference. Explain, "The treble clef is also called the G clef. See how circles begin to grow around the G line. If you forget where the notes are, always look for the G line and tap your pencil point on the illustrated G line extension. Continue to prompt, "Look for the G line," until fluency is ingrained. *Do not* continue teaching past page 25 in this book. At this point, move the lessons into the *Alfred's Basic Piano Series* (see the explanation of this method at the end of this chapter).

The Alfred Basic Piano Series

The student is now ready to begin with the *Alfred's Basic Piano Series*. The Alfred series combines the *Lesson, Recital, Theory,* and *Technic* books, starting with level 1A. This works every time. At this point, the student has developed enough technique to advance to sight-reading, which is in sync with the speed of the student's progress. In Alfred Book 1A, notes are introduced in the C position, followed by the G position. At this point, the student already has experience with this level of complexity.

The payoff of this approach begins to show right from the start. The fingering is perfect, the hand-eye coordination is developed, the fine motor control and motor planning is refining, the visual tracking has expanded, and your student is comfortable in the position he's playing in. He has to focus on just one thing: identifying the notes on the page, and he already knows where those notes are on the keyboard.

Lesson 1

1. The first lesson is in the *Lesson Book,* pages 30–31 (right hand only).
2. Reinforce the concept of the G line.
    a. See illustration on the top of that page in the book.
    b. Refer to the G line as the "second line from the bottom, in the treble clef." With a pencil, extend the G line a bit outward to the left, and write the letter G next to it.

3. Also introduce pages 4 and 5 in the *Technic Book*. Have the student play *only* the treble clef parts (A. Double Plays; B. Triple Plays; C. Hold It; and D. Four to Go!). You'll introduce the bass clef at the next lesson.
4. Next, from the *Recital Book,* teach *Gee We're Glad,* the first treble-clef song on page 12.
    a. In this song, the student begins to learn flexibility with the notes, especially as it begins with the G line and works its way down in stepwise motion. This is a giant leap for new readers, but well timed for this point of the lesson.
    b. Some students have trouble counting the alphabet backwards, so it needs to be penciled in near the title of the until they learn how to do it independently. *Never write the names of the notes above the notes in the assignment.*
5. Assign these songs (just introduced) as the assignment for practice until the next lesson.
6. Since the student has just learned the right-hand notes in *My Piano Book A,* beginning with these songs serves to reinforce his learning.

If possible, also add some theory. This is a time to adjust the amount of free time in the lesson and begin to include theory. As the student develops in her technique, you want to reinforce what she is learning in the corresponding books in the series. This establishes balanced musicianship right from the start.

Lesson 2

1. Go backwards now, and return to pages 28–29 in the *Lesson Book*.
2. Introduce the F Line.
    a. See the illustration on the top of that page in the book.
    b. Explain the F line as "the second line from the top in the bass clef." With a pencil, extend the F line a bit outward to the left, and write the letter "F" next to it.

3. Explain, "The bass clef is also called the F clef, because the two dots wrap around the F line."
4. Direct the student to use the left hand when she sees the bass/F clef.
5. Next, return to the songs from the last lesson (pages 4–5 in the *Technic Book*). Mark the F clef, and have the student play the left-hand parts for the two songs on the page.

Lesson 3
1. Discuss page 32 in the *Lesson Book*.
2. Introduce the grand staff. "There are all these notes on the grand staff."
   a. Demonstrate how the notes on the page correspond with the keys on the piano.
3. On page 33, the student should begin to play from the grand staff, both clefs simultaneously, albeit one clef at a time.
   a. The book keeps it simple, so that only one hand is playing at any given time in the song. This is the time to return to page 4 in the *Technic Book,* and play the songs on the page.
4. Continue on to pages 34–35, and reinforce the grand staff note reading and tracking from the F and G lines.
5. Important: Under-assign rather than over-assign, to keep your students motivated. If you over-assign, they become overwhelmed. Often, the student will ask for more work when he recognizes his abilities.

Continuing Lessons

The Lesson Book remains the core book. For each assignment, make sure to pay careful attention to the corresponding pages for other books in the series, as referenced on the topmost corner of the page. For example, when the student reaches page 34, *A Happy Song,* it's time to also teach the corresponding page in the *Recital Book,* which has a small note on page 13 indicating that this song (*Christopher Columbus*) should be taught only after *A Happy Song* is taught from page 34 in the *Lesson Book*. And so you continue the lessons, with the corresponding books each time.

Important Notes
1. The *Technic* and *Recital* and *Theory* books reinforce everything introduced in the *Lesson Book*. This is how the series is laid out. It's important to incorporate all of these other books so that the student absorbs the information in its entirety. Skipping the *Theory* books will impede the student's understanding of why things are written as they are, such as key signatures, dynamics, and fundamentals of music.
2. Some younger students may need parental assistance for handwriting or until their motor issues progress via occupational therapy. Fine motor skills also improve while playing piano, speeding up this milestone.
3. If the student is extremely slow in her note reading comprehension skills, the *Fun Book* in the same series is another reinforcer. This usually solves the problem and gets her reading proficiently.

Solfege and Intervals Training

Thanks to the familiar song, "Do, A Deer" (which is maddeningly sung in Bb in the *Sound of Music*) students have a basic understanding of solfege. Oftentime, the piano teacher will focus on technique and note-reading, and overlook solfege in their teaching. The objective for the teacher should be to instill well-rounded musicianship skills to enhance the student's self-esteem so they can belong in the world of music-making, no matter where they go in their future. Many start with piano lessons, and then branch out into other instruments, composing, or music business and sound recording technology. It all starts with the early teaching, and that is in the hands of the piano teacher. The students has only one chance to be captivated by music as a whole, and the teacher must employ all strategies to best tap into the student's learning style while still motivated. If the student fails, they will be turned off from all parts of music, forever, and also left with a bad taste in association to anything music-related.

We constantly hear parents tell us, "If I had been taught piano in this way, I would've stuck with it." We also hear stories of regret, failure, and humiliation from parents who quit lessons or school band because they were made to believe that they were to stupid to get with program, or simply not talented. Susan's mother was asked to leave her school's children's choir because she was told she could not sing. She actually had relative pitch, and they probably sang in a vocal range that was not physically possible for her, and therefore brought out the worst in her performance. This is very common where directors are sticking to a curriculum that is designed for a small minority, and are unable to transpose to meet the needs of their students, who are a small minority in the bigger picture of music-making.

It is Henny's preference to introduce solfege at the time the student transition into G position with the Alfred series. Susan prefers to skip solfege entirely, since it was her experience that it is an unnecessary layer of complexity with piano playing, since she was trained as a pianist in the classical tradition, she never heard of Solfege until college. In Henny's case, her first introduction to music fundamentals was in college, where she first learned solfege before letter-names, it continued to serve a different purpose in her musicianship. At that time, Henny was able to see the notes, and sing it (seeing it meant she heard it in her head) and it frustrated her that she was being forced to label those sounds in an organized language that was alien to her. Henny hears pitch in solfege, while Susan hears them as letter names. Henny is captivated with choral singing, while Susan, being an instrumentalist, is not. In either case, here are some important strategies for bringing in solfege as a positive tool that may be essential to the student's long-term musicianship.

In the beginning of note-reading, the Alfred series will introduce *seconds* and *thirds* as harmonies for the left hand. The students quickly learn that the two notes (some call it the 'twins') will need to be played simultaneously. The visual stacking of sounds matches the intervals they hear in their head. When they play it, they have an extraordinary sense of power, hearing the huge sound they are instantly able to create. Henny's favorite part of teaching is watching the student play "Quiet River", which is the first time they are putting both hands together while also trying to play *legato*. Seeing the faces of recognized accomplishment is a beautiful thing.

For the first lesson in G position, Henny uses the following language:

- "Under the title of the song, please write this sentence with your pencil: Do, spelled D-O, Re, spelled R-E, Mi, spelled M-I, Fa, spelled F-A, and Sol, spelled S-O- with a silent L".
- Now, under this sentence, put in parenthesis this word: Solfege, spelled S-O-L-F-E-G-E".
- Solfege is a universal language for teaching notes without the alphabet. Imagine your friends in China, or your friends in Israel. They don't have "C-D-E" in their language. So, the first note becomes the Do (wiggle your thumb). The next one becomes the Mi, and so on.
- So tell me, look at the song here. We are in G position now, so we will begin to read from the G line. So that first G, that's going to be your Do. What is the next note? It's okay to 'cheat' and refer to the chart you have made for yourself on top of the page.

At this point, the students will realize that, not only did they solfege their first song, but several other skills occurred:

- They flawlessly transitioned into G position
- They are using their interval skills of counting seconds, thirds, fourths, or fifths, to skip between solfege.
- They unknowingly sing the solfege in the correct pitch, rather than speaking/naming them.
- They no longer think in letters, but rather, think in intervals.

The last point is the primary objective to prove that the neurological pathways have been established for associative rather than pitch-based thinking. To ingrain a skill of visual discrimination is critical for moving a absolute pitcher from the piecemeal thinking to the greater whole. At this point, most absolute pitch students will profess to be able to look at the song, and 'hear' the whole thing. This cannot happen in the previous books (Keyboard Talent Hunt), because the books is forcing them to break the musical concepts into tiny building blocks. Students will often mumble while playing, "a G and a D, then, a C and an F …", reading the two lines simultaneously. When they learn the intervals in the Alfred Series, all vocalization disappears, and the eye becomes the strongest guide for the playing. The eye-tracking is complete, and the dependence on the notes is permanent.

At this point, nonverbal students tend to become more fluent in their typed communication, and have sustained eye-tracking and focus that lasts for the entire lesson. Also, by now, students have been made aware of their gift, since they have been tested several times for perfect pitch with the piano matching method. They are aware of their strengths, and have probably already mentioned their gifts to someone important in their lives. Their confidence is high now, because they are note-reading, and there is no trauma involved in this joyous journey.

After the student finishes sight-singing their first song, Henny likes to follow up this momentous occasion with, "Congratulations! You just sight-sang your first song!" and sometimes add, "Most music majors can't do that!" This is an important moment to acknowledge their musicianship, and Henny often shares her back-story on this. Growing up in New York City, it was always her childhood dream to ride the subway and learn a new song just from reading the score. She had once seen someone do that, and it has captivated her for more than 30 years until she learned how to do it. Obsessed with the skill, she yearns to teach that to every last person on the planet.

Henny guides the students in fine-tuning their ear to sing *seconds* and *thirds* intervals (do-re, do-mi), now that they know what they look like on the page. She suggests that the student should "play a C, then sing a D in your head, the sing an E out loud". Students get to play the E to test themselves. They are usually shocked that they got it right on the first try. At that point, their assignment is to sing in the shower, shamelessly, or when waiting for the schoolbus. "Practice all these skips and steps and you will see how your accuracy increases every time". Students love the little song that Henny plays, pressing a C continuously as a drone, playing C-D, C-E, C-F, etc., while singing, "A Second, a Third, a Fourth, a Fifth, a Fourth, a Third, a Second, and back home". Students develop the confidence to sing "A Fifth" over time, when they practice skipping inside their heads, and singing out with confidence into the requested interval. This is a very rewarding exercise for those who adore singing and want to advance their musicianship into other realms. For non-speaking students, the parent is instructed to write the first five solfege words on a paper. The parent is instructed to point to the note on the page, and the student is instructed to points to the solfege that they think it is. Henny guides by saying, "The first one is the Do. So now, what's the next one?"

Practice

You assign a new song each week, and caution the parent never to play it for the student, since he will reproduce the sound rather than sight-read. He is just mimicking what's being played, feeding into the auditory strengths. Therefore he's asked to practice his pieces three times each, for three days a week. No time is set, because to him, thirty minutes feels like thirty hours. Since students of all cognitive levels can count to three, this schedule is easily explained and added into the student's weekly planning. Remind the student that the more they practice, they better they get.

For AP individuals, it's important not to spend an enormous amount of time practicing the same songs over and over again. A high level of boredom can result from tedious practicing. The absolute pitcher compensates by playing from auditory memory rather than note reading. This undermines the learning benefits of the reading practice. Additionally, spacing out the practice in regular intervals (once every day rather than three times every other day) allows the brain to absorb the information and make the new skills permanent.

Sticking to the 3 × 3 practice formula seems to be the key to unlocking steady progress toward successful sight-reading. Adherence to this formula is vital, since the journey of strengthening the visual processing is crucial and is accessible only in this way. If you question your student on her practice habits and she tells you that she spent only ten minutes last week practicing, please understand that AP students can practice mentally in their heads wherever they are, with or without a piano.

The Alfred series 1B follows by reinforcing the C and then G positions, which were already introduced in the 1A series. At this point, there's more of the same, but the songs add a level of flexibility from C to G position and review those positions. The book then introduces the middle C position and starts to bridge positions together. Students do well with this level, and don't struggle with bridging positions.

The Alfred Series Level 2 books bridge more of the notes together, and the fingering becomes more intricate. This book is on a much more challenging level than what your students have seen until now. If they can make it through this level, then the rest of the series is very achievable and rewarding. This is the hardest set in the series because so much new bridging is introduced. By the time they get to level 3, they've had a lot of experience in bridging notes together and learning new notes and technique, and are really enjoying themselves. It continues this way until all six levels of the series have been studied.

A question parents often ask is "Why doesn't the book have songs that my kid knows?" There's a reason for that. If he knows the song, then he plays it by ear and doesn't read the music. By doing songs that he's unfamiliar with, he has to read the music and learn to read notes. Outside of the lesson, he can go to the music store and pick up music for songs that are familiar to him. Though he won't play them correctly at this level of his training, he'll feel confident in his ability to read, with enough guesstimation, to produce something that gives him pleasure. You can include those songs as a reward in the lessons.

The right time to assessing for AP during this journey of instruction depends on a few things. First, it depends on the parents' accounts of the child's independent musical forays. Very prodigious absolute pitchers often play tirelessly, pushing their boundaries and delighting their families. The teacher's observations of behavior and characteristic traits lends to the intuition on when to test. Susan usually tests in the middle of the *Keyboard Talent Hunt Book 2* in the C position.

Teaching Strategies

Transition – Your student might struggle with transitioning into the session. Those with AP will most likely run to an instrument and begin to play their personal ditty. This should be allowed, uninterrupted, and be recognized as the individual's technique for self-regulation.

Extreme AP'ers might prefer to go on for a long time since they have a need to demonstrate their abilities in a form of communication that they have now mastered. After a few minutes, you can begin to prompt for a countdown. Also, watch for bodily clues, as a change in demeanor will become apparent in time. While playing a melody, some individuals might tolerate headphones for electronic keyboards, allowing them to stim on loud, obnoxious sounds such as a rapid beat with lots of chords. Offer headphones, but don't push for their use just because the sound is too loud for you. Rather, give the student the space she needs in order to enter your space.

Routine – Always start with the student playing his or her assigned piece first. Then, give her the choice of instruments and songs for free time. Once she learns the routine of the session, she understands what's expected and will come in doing exactly what she's asked to do. She becomes very comfortable, and then it isn't a challenge for either of you. Part of it is setting up piano as the first thing you do, so that she understands which part is work and which is the reward. With kids who have trouble making choices, use a choices picture board at the start of the session. Say, "After piano, we can do …" and let them make an informed choice for later.

Presentation – How you present the information to the client is the predictor of the outcome. You must remember to keep pointing at all times to the note that he or she needs to play. This is to accommodate his or her visual processing and eye tracking weaknesses.

When the student drops his head, you continue pointing, so that when he or she finally brings his head up to look and see what's next, you're right there for him or her. Every absolute pitcher does this. It's how they're wired and they are not to be reprimanded for it. We're there just to try to make their journey easier.

Experiment with presenting the sheet music on an iPad, on which your client can enlarge or shrink the music as he needs to. The iPad has the added bonus of adjustable lighting, and sometimes even the background color of the page is adjustable.

Be aware that electronic keyboards sometimes situate the sheet music stand farther away from the eyes than on acoustic pianos. Recognize that the change in perspective might throw your client off track and disorient him or her. You can incorporate some ingenious tools, such as attaching the music to extendable wall mirrors whose arms can be adjusted to the precise distance needed.

To help with visual processing, experiment with placing the music book flat on the piano top, or at different angles, for maximum comfort. As your client's exertion and anxiety increase during the work, adjustments will have to be made to sustain the flow and engage his or her strengths.

Body Behaviors – Self-stimulatory behaviors, also known as stimming, are a very important part of the individual's life. From the outside, it's difficult to judge whether his or her body movements are in his or her control or not. Lest you jump to erroneous conclusions, it's crucial to understand the cause of the movement. Every stim is a result of the brain trying to communicate and make things work. For an individual with sensory issues, his or her brain struggles to make sense of the very basic sensory stimuli that you take for granted each day.

In your own studio, you might not be aware of the wall clock ticking, the fluorescent bulb that flickers, or the light fixture that buzzes. For example, Susan's client, R, refused to play the F key on the acoustic piano. Although she was only five years old, she knew enough to say, "I not like dis F." She had no problem playing the F on the electronic keyboard. When the piano tuner came a few weeks later, Susan asked him to check the acoustic F. Peering inside, he revealed that the strings to the left of the F were all steel, while the strings on the right side of that F were all copper. That particular F and its neighboring F# were both silver. The timbre of these 2 strings were very different from the rest of the strings.

It is important to listen to clients and hear them out. They are telling you something, either with their words or with their resistance. Respect that their sensitivity is at a level that defies your comprehension. Without imagining it, believe it and accommodate accordingly. Making your studio a sensory-friendly environment might necessitate hiring an autistic adult to do a quick sensory audit for you.

Tools that you can purchase are available for cheap. Keep a few Koosh balls and 1¼-inch hedge balls (also called porcupine balls) scattered above the piano. If the client needs to, he or she will reach out for one, use it, then let go when he or she is done. Another ingenious idea is to buy a grass bath mat that has soft plastic bristles. Put one on the piano bench and another on the floor near the pedals. Ask the student to remove his or her socks and shoes if he or she didn't when he or she first arrived. You might refer to these devices as the "magic carpet," the "concentration balls," or some other dignified terms that make them okay to use.

Make an extra effort to keep the odors of your home cooking out of the studio space. Buy hand soap and bathroom supplies that have no dyes or perfumes. Use unscented deodorizers rather than air fresheners with synthetic scents. Respect that an odor which the student can't place might drive her nuts and make it very difficult for her to function. Not every student will be able to ask, "What's that smell?!" Offer such information as "By the way, I'm preparing chicken for dinner, in case you're smelling it."

If you work in a school, recognize that the student might smell the food from the cafeteria throughout the building. Be understanding about the plumbing for the radiators and bathrooms contained inside the walls. The sounds of those pipes working, the water moving through them, can seem extra-loud for people with overly receptive senses.

Temple Grandin describes the recess bell as a dentist's drill hitting a nerve. Be respectful of this heightened sensitivity. Keep doors closed when possible, shades drawn to reduce sunlight, and lights dimmed or off. Don't use lamps to compensate. Instead, consider skylights or large lighting fixtures concealed within the woodwork. Ask your client if a particular lamp is okay. Monitor her behaviors afterward to see if her abilities became reduced, even if she was unaware of it.

Avoid using large mirrors, even when training for voice. The student will struggle with eye contact and it will be unbearable for her to look at her mouth when her eyes are right there in her face. If you must, use a small hand mirror so that only the student's mouth is reflected.

Flexibility – Autistic students can benefit from being asked to use one inverted chord once per improvisation. This encourages flexibility in a musical way in which the change is rewarded aurally. "Shaking up" a routine can be very difficult, but in music, habits are much easier to break away from so as to develop flexibility. This is where improvisation comes into your teaching. The fabulous music of the improvisation takes precedence over repeating old routines. You don't have to do the same song or the same instruments each week. Respect that your client is making the choice, no matter what it is. Through the reward of the sound, he'll be encouraged to be more flexible and explore greater variety. Getting him to use his voice, and to see that he *has* a voice to connect, helps him use something that might previously have been trapped inside him.

For extreme right-brained AP'ers, producing a melody occurs when the sound of the song is played effortlessly with the right hand. The left-hand pinkie finger intuitively traces the coordinating sound. The untrained student might be unable to explain why she chose an A major chord to go with a melody in that key. She just goes there. Thus chords in root position are very natural, since the 1-3-5 pattern is easy to apply and songs can be played instantly. For a typical left brainer, 3+6 is always nine, as is 6+3, because of the formula it belongs to. For a right-brainer who has yet to tap into left-brain functions (which occurs after significant training), 3+6 is always nine. But when you turn that around to 6+3, she will interpret it literally and have to compute all over again.

Inverted chords therefore make no sense to such an untrained thinker, since inversion confuses the "mind" of the pinkie finger. The student gets lost, and cannot understand why E-C-A is the same as A-C-E. On the other hand, introducing a right-brained AP'er to simple chord progressions is remarkable. She hears it once and she gets it right away. The sound is a pattern she can understand, rather than grasping the theory as a formula.

When teaching I-IV-V progressions to a left-brainer, he'll be able to tell you what the IV of any key is by playing the scale on the piano. A right-brainer will answer the question simply by playing the chord in root position on the keyboard; the sound tells him if it's correct or not. In other words, he knows the sound of the IV, even if he can't tell you exactly why he played a specific note sharp or flat. Simplify inversions by saying that you are merely changing the order of the chord. Once the APer is shown the concept, they can relate the visual-tactile to the auditory.

Using Various Mediums – It's helpful to use picture books during improvisation if your client has trouble articulating something in the song. For example, have pictures of the farm animals handy when singing *Old MacDonald*. Picture storybooks help your client visualize the concept if she's having trouble comprehending the meaning from the lyrics.

Biting – Students sometimes randomly bite others in their space. While biting is a normal behavior in development, it typically disappears after age four. In autistic people, completion of the sensorimotor stage of childhood can take a long time. If a student bites you, it might appear that she was unprovoked and acted at random. Understand that she is still in the sensorimotor stage, learning by touching, feeling, mouthing. Since you entered her line of vision, in order for her to know what you are and what you're doing, he or she had to touch or lick or bite you. The hope is that your student will develop some sense of the environment so he or she needs to touch less often. For now, stimming provides the input from an alternate place, which eliminates the need for information to be learned orally.

Exaggeration – Take the time to over-dramatize your expressions and nonverbal gestures. When singing, *There Was an Old Lady Who Swallowed a Fly,* you should moan and groan as the lady's troubles multiply in the story.

Silliness – Being silly is very important. Even when your client has trouble veering from literal perception, modeling silliness as an adult makes it okay for him or her to step into that abstract world. For older students, it's okay to be silly when they make mistakes while sight-reading. You can add casual humor into your comments. For older clients, such as seniors with dementia, a rubber ducky breaks the ice and creates a connection.

Resistance to Change – In her book *The Way I See It,* Temple Grandin writes that autistic individuals associate a trauma with the context in which it occurred rather than with the cause of the trauma. Grandin compares it to a dog that gets hit by a truck, and then associates the pain with that spot on the road rather than with the vehicle. If your client hears you play a song and your guitar suddenly goes out of tune, he might associate the pain of that sound (which is magnified for him) with your studio. This is not an extreme example but a typical occurrence. If your light bulbs flicker or buzz, your client might resist ever again entering your office.

When you've made a change in your setup—had the carpets cleaned, added a new couch cushion, or recently had the piano tuned—inform your client in advance. Being caught unaware instantly triggers his or her associating the trauma of change with your studio. Being informed helps him or her arrive at a place of calm as he or she works through it in advance.

Sensory Overload – If the client stays outside your door and refuses to enter, go outside to work with her. You need to be where she is, wherever she's coming from. Bring the marimba to the door. Start to play it and sing, and try to engage her. Have a set of mallets for her. At least when he or she hears you, you can engage him or her by drawing her in through the sound. Sometimes, you can engage the parents by handing them the mallets. This establishes a comfort level so they don't feel out of place, especially if you're a new person in their lives.

Next, think about what changed in your room, and inform him or her. If the client is already overloaded from the highway sounds during the car ride, she might not be able to tolerate the sounds of your environment even if he or she's always tolerated them in the past. For this reason alone, a Skype session is an advantage for competent clinicians, as it eliminates the client's travel, potential overload, and any transition issues. Also, the client is in control, and can shut you off from his or her space with one click.

Instead of bright over-head lights, offer a dark and quiet space, free of people, where the client can recalibrate his or her sensory systems. This is easily provided by turning off all lights, drawing the shades in the room, and shutting down all sounds such as a keyboard's power button. Be aware of the little lights on power cords, alarm clocks, and computers. Open your door again and gesture toward the sanctum. Most clients will prefer to regroup without anyone present.

Taking It Literally – Your students may have the tendency to take everything you say very literally. You can never say something like "Oops—that was a wrong note." In his or her mind, that's like a giant hammer that just bopped him or her on the head with permanent impact. The meaning is magnified, and he or she can instantly feel like a failure. Just like the girl with the curl, he or she can only remember when he or she was bad, so tone down your feedback so as to focus on the positive. Rather than remark on what didn't happen, just switch that around to "You're going to want to put your thumb on the C. There, try it again." When a student plays a wrong note, just say the word "close" or "not quite."

In an effort to be kind, we try to be extra-nice to people and ask them ever so sweetly, "Honey, can you please take out the trash?" An autistic student who is asked to do something with a "can you?" might ignore, not respond, or just simply answer, "Yes." Yes, he or she can. He or she is thinking, "Oh, wait, you want me to do that? Oh." Just erase the "Can you?" and remember that *direct* is the root of the word "directions." Just give a direction. It's not rude—it's necessary.

Like their typical peers, some autistic children have very vivid imaginations, and some do not. Tap into dormant imagery by incorporating puppets or toy animals. These interactive creatures make it safe to have a "conversation" in which mistakes are okay. Once inhibitions are removed, generalizing to real human interaction is freer to carry over. With puppets, it's important to talk about the puppet so that third-person thoughts and feelings are revealed indirectly. This takes the pressure off of the client to interact with direct references, making it safe for an individual with language differences to articulate more freely, since he or she isn't talking about him or herself in first person. To create a safe environment, ask, "What is the horse doing?"

"He's jumping."

Immediately, acknowledge that by singing, "The horse is jumping, he's jumping in the ____" and so on. This stimulates conversation and imagination.

Validate, Validate, Validate – Let your student know that he or she is not the only one having trouble in this area. It is important for him or her to know that it's normal to struggle with piano; that so many typical people don't succeed at it. Let him or her know how strong he or she is for persevering and working through the challenges and rewards that piano has to offer. It's one of the most difficult instruments, and his or her determination needs to be acknowledged.

Teaching Guitar

Start with one-finger chords. On the lowest string, at the third fret, place the first (index) finger on the string while strumming the four bottom strings. For the C chord, use the first finger on the first fret, second string, and strum the four bottom strings. The full D7 chord is taught next, by placing the first finger on the first fret, second string, the second finger up on the third string, second fret, and the third finger on the sixth string, second fret. D7 can be strummed with the five bottom strings, or just four strings to eliminate confusion at this level. These three early chords are taught for their simplicity, making the transition easy when the full G chord is introduced.

For AP students, your aim is to show them how easy guitar is for accompanying the voice. By starting with chords rather than sight-reading, you empower students to accompany themselves easily from the start. As more and more chords are taught each week, the theory becomes ingrained in the I-IV-V concepts, and the AP student will be delighted to discover how easy it is to transpose on guitar. Ideas for different strum patterns are introduced, at which point the student is very motivated to plow through them at a rapid pace, increasing her proficiency each day. If a student needs familiar repertoire to practice their chords, you may bring back the *Keyboard Talent Hunt* Book 2 and have them sing the melodies. The left hand notes can serve as a guide for their chords, where C--- is a C chord, and G--- is a G chord.

After chords are explored and the student's repertoire is enriched by her accompaniment skills, finger picking is taught. For the student with visual-processing weaknesses, the guitar design offers a way to make music without looking at the fingers, which are a great visual distraction. At this point, the student's technique is refined enough to introduce sight-reading, in which she can keep her eyes on the page and not need to refer back to the instrument to check their fingering.

AP students should be complimented and reminded of their gift as they tune their guitars by ear before and during lessons. When this ability is highlighted, the student will develop the confidence to show that off to her peers, earning respect from seasoned musicians. In contrast, if you introduce AP students to sight-reading (for guitar) first, they get bored and quit. Playing classical melodies written for the guitar might not provide the rich and full sound that an absolute pitcher so craves; therefore offering volume through chords excites the student to continue the journey of learning.

In the tuning instruction, you might introduce the client to the silly tuning acronym "Ernie Ate Dynamite, Good Bye Ernie." Then proceed to explain, "We will now learn the first three strings, which are also *Good Bye Ernie.*" Start with the *Guitar Method Grade 1* book (Mel

Bay Publishing). On the first day, work with "Notes On The E String" on pages 7–8.

Upon his return the next week, test the client to see whether he can sing E-F-G while playing. He might not understand unless you do it first. This is the beginning of connecting letters while playing, which then connects letters to notes, which in turn connects letters to sound when reading the notes. Many clients can then soar with that discovery and suddenly sight-sing without further ado. It's important to know at this point whether the client has autism or math and reading-comprehension issues in school. Those with intense RBAP or autism will be unable to connect a random concept such as a finger having a number, or a sound having a letter. By using the Rancer Method, the left brain will begin to be activated in this process, and the client will develop the skill for naming fingers or notes. This takes a long time, and sight-reading consistently without calling it by a name or enforcing finger numbers is the key here. It's helpful for many to rest the pinkie finger on the guitar body so the hand doesn't lose its place. We want to encourage the client not to look at her hands, so bracing her hand this way allows her to look away and at the notes.

If you stick to this method from the start, you'll notice a magical response: The client will be able to follow from sight-reading and fly through the notes without even being able to name them. Continue in the next lesson (page 9) for "Notes On the B String." Again, just show the client how the notes go up or down, and so do the fingers and so does the sound. For the songs on page 10, the client will need a refresher of the original notes for the first string. You might want to highlight the staff lines for E and B in two different colors, signaling the open strings. This way, the client knows. "This is my first open string, and this is my second open string, and I need to work up or down from that reference point."

You then sit patiently while he struggles through playing the songs that include both strings. Once he cracks this, the magic has begun. In the next lesson, introduce "Notes On the G String" (page 11). At this point, the client will delight in playing the first example song, because he has the sight-reading skills to plow through most of the staff line.

At this point, it's important to compliment the client on her newly developed guitar calluses. Explain it as the ultimate badge of honor. Remind them to show it off to their friends. For adults, coach them on proper care for maintaining those calluses, such as not playing after a shower when the calluses are soft, lest they tear. Acknowledging that only a lot of hard work earns one the calluses is also an acknowledgment of how much they've been practicing.

Over the next week, you might learn that the client has been composing, or exploring the instrument some more. Encourage them to record it. Try to assess their desire to write it down, and see if they can play and notate, which is a reverse-order process. At this point, very casually mention letter names and weave them into their expressions through musical channels. This is where you can begin to push the boundaries of the instrument—to the client's delight. It's critical to continue to enforce "looking away" so that visual processing continues to be exercised. Otherwise, the client avoids reading and feeds right into the sound source, a very primal RBAP behavior that should be undone.

At this point, you may want to introduce the piano for the purpose of teaching the lower notes on the staff via the Rancer Method. The most important reason for introducing piano at this point is to ingrain the theory using the linear instrument. Once the client has learned enough theory through songs using a I-IV-V progression in several keys, he is now ready pick out his favorite harmonies on the guitar.

Chapter Seven

Accommodating The Individual Gift

> *To be disciplined is to follow in a good way.*
> *To be self-disciplined, is to follow in a better way.*
> —John Cage

Not everyone learns by ear. Parents are in charge of the delicate work of shaping their child into a functional and successful adult while tending to their basic needs at the same time. This might be a paradox. As you cater to your child's need, you wonder if you're teaching dependence. If you don't have the same needs your child has, it can be difficult to sort out how much is too much and when it turns into bending over backwards till you break. Yet parents of children with special needs have no problem accommodating. They simply study the needs, grow with their child, and adapt.

Educators face that same challenge. Do we allow the student with a convergence disorder to be eligible for audio textbooks? How will he or she learn to read? Yet that determination should not be at the discretion of the teacher. If an individual is eligible for an accommodation that helps him or her do as well as his or her peers, then the experts who've studied the need made that determination long ago. The answer is yes. That individual should definitely have his or her textbooks on audio. Over time, he or she will learn to read through other therapies, but not if he or she is under pressure to catch up with his or her peers' reading level in time for the next class. Using the audio will help him stay on track. We owe our students the dignity of finding a way to help them do well by capitalizing on their strengths.

When an older adult first learns what absolute pitch means, he or she can become quite emotional. For the first time in his or her life, he or she has the shocking awareness that other people "don't have this." What we most often hear when the person regains his or her composure is: "You mean other people can't do it?" It's hard to fathom a life without the systems that work for you. In society, we have tremendous respect for the person who navigates the world despite being blind. The reason we respect him or her for that is because we believe we couldn't do it if we closed our own eyes for a time. Yet the blind person doesn't know what he or she is missing—this is all he or she has ever known. It's just a part of his or her life and part of who he or she is. For a person with absolute pitch, harmonizing the first time he or she hears a song is normal. Playing back something he or she just heard is as natural as breathing.

For a teacher who doesn't have absolute pitch, this is beyond comprehension. Aristotle said, "It is the mark of an educated mind to be able to entertain a thought without accepting it." For example, the traditional teacher will teach the notes on the staff using age-old mnemonics such as "Every Good Boy Does Fine" or "F-A-C-E" for the lines and spaces. For auditory learners, these are counterproductive to learning, because their brain process is entirely the reverse of that of visual learners.

Assessing for Absolute Pitch

Absolute pitch is not learned; it's inborn. The AP is always present, but the individual must first possess the skills to be tested. Frequent testing is therefore necessary for the beginning student so that AP can be diagnosed accurately.

Caution: Students who have no introduction to music at all will be difficult to test. Give careful attention to such students when you teach them for the purpose of testing. The Rancer Method specifically highlights the learning steps when a student should be assessed.

First, look for the following clues in the student:

- Does he sing in pitch?
- Does she transpose octave to octave to match your pitch?
- Does he have a good sense of rhythm?
- Does she get upset when you change the key of a piece or put in a wrong chord?
- Can he imitate rhythm and pitch patterns?
- Does she correct herself while reading the piece for the first time?
- Can the student play a song with minimal chords on the Qchord?
- Can he complete a song that you started on the tone bells?
- Does she pick out notes by ear on the tone bells?
- Does he harmonize while singing with others or recordings?
- Does she cover her ears while you try to harmonize with her (or cringe, or short-stop singing)?
- Does he try to play the same note you do on his violin while you strum and sing on the guitar?
- Does she sing the pitch you were first singing after you try to change the key of a piece?
- Does he grab the guitar (or lunge at your instrument) when you intentionally play the wrong chord?
- Does she refuse to play along with you because she can't play the instrument with enough accuracy to match your pitch?
- Does he get easily frustrated because he's not playing to his standard of perfection?

- Does she want you to play her (string) instrument so she can hear the correct pitch?
- Bach – they either love it or hate it.
- Can he easily reproduce a song he just heard, and match up harmonies in the left hand on the piano without thinking in theory such as I-IV-V?
- Can she dial a phone number without knowing the numbers by heart?
- Does he know when he pressed an incorrect number on the phone keypad by hearing its tone?
- Can she sing back the melody of people's phone numbers?

Even more clues:
- Nearly all AP/RPs have a musical ditty that they play before they start working, as a warm-up.
- Adults without AP, including musicians and nonmusicians, consistently sing familiar songs starting on the same absolute pitch as the original recording.[9]
- Experiments showed that AP possessors could judge whether a musical excerpt was played in the correct key at significantly above-chance levels.[10]

Non-Verbal Testing Method
- AP and RP seem to almost always be testable in the *Keyboard Talent Hunt* book by Schaum Publications.
- Once the letter names are learned and there's ease in playing. This is the time to begin testing for AP or RP. To test in the

---

[9] Halpern, A. R. (1989). Memory for the absolute pitch of familiar songs. *Memory & Cognition,* 17, 572-581.

[10] Terhardt, E., & Seewann, M. (1983). Aural key identification and its relationship to absolute pitch. *Music Perception,* 1, 63-83.; Terhardt, E., & Ward, W. D. (1982). Recognition of musical key: Exploratory study. *Journal of the Acoustical Society of America,* 72, 26-33.

C position is the easiest for them, because it's the first thing they've learned.
- Place the student's right hand in the C position.
- Then you, the tester, should be seated at a nearby piano, your hands hidden by a large book.
- Play a note on the piano, and ask the student to match the note on her piano. For best results, ask the student to look at his or her hands during the test. (Always test on the same instrument the student is learning on.)
- Eventually, do a cold testing without auditory clues to make your test most accurate.

Eye tracking – Observe the student's eyes when he reads music. He might actively process every note in each measure, one at a time, top to bottom, seeing a logical mathematical sequence in how they align. Or, he will scan the page, often losing his place, and you can see the eye hovering above the melody's contour. You might want to video-record the lesson to observe these traits later.

Such students fake to please, seeking a clue to the melody line, guessing at the sound from the wavy shape of the notes. In other words, the eye either goes in strict left-to-right motion or it hovers over the contour line as it moves left to right. When reading books, these students' eyes might be scanning the shapes of words rather than absorbing the individual letters. For a visual teacher, this behavior is difficult to understand: "The music is right in front of her—why doesn't she just play the notes?"

These individuals do better when reading narrow columns, which allow the eye to recall where to return to for the next line after tracking across the page. When you sing for a young client with a picture book, observe if he first tracks the words and then the pictures, or if he wanders around the page taking in the whole scene. The former indicates a visual learner who will sight-read well, the latter an auditory learner who'll struggle with sight-reading.

This is remedied with eye exercises; a developmental pediatrician should make a referral to an optometrist who specializes in convergence insufficiencies and visual-perception differences. The child's parents will thank you, and your professional image will soar, putting you on the level of the professionals you referred them to. When the student returns for her lessons wearing customized prism glasses or Irlen lenses, these issues gradually vanish.

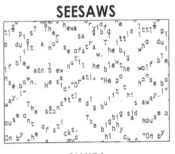

Sample visual distortions of letters on a page

Fingering – Left-brained visual learners (LBAPs) will readjust their fingers by moving the whole hand to the new placement as they read the notes and map out the sequence of the next measure. Right-brained aural learners (RBAPs) will trip fingers over each other carelessly, or even turn the whole hand over to produce the next sound in their heads. When reproducing, improvising, or transposing, LBAPs' eyes look intently at the fingers as they mathematically use music theory to move up or down stepwise or intervallically. RBAPs' eyes look up and away so that nothing gets in the way of getting out the sound.

RBAPs also use only one or two fingers, so that the fingers don't get in the way either. Such students will enter your studio and head straight to the piano, plunking out a song with just their index fingers. Most early AP students will begin by playing melodies by ear with their right hand first. Some never use the left hand in improvisation. These abilities are highly individualized and do not correlate with the individual's' level of AP. However, if a student improvises freely with both hands (without training), then they are very prodigious from the outset. The genetic memory of the ability is a part of this process, and is layered with their early exposure of cultural and specific genre. Typically, the student will use the right hand to play the melody, while the left hand might reveal to be more prodigious in the long run. This can be linked to right-side processing weakness with sensory-integration disorders, and especially motor planning.

Your Language

The visual learner looks at a word in a book and associates meaning by processing the letters and referring to a previously stored concept for each letter in his memory bank. The auditory learner looks at the word as a whole and attaches the shape of the word to a meaning, the shape having been previously stored in his memory bank. When studying music, the visual learner processes every note individually. The auditory learner derives meaning by observing the shape of the melody as judged by the rise and fall of the notes across the line. These fundamental differences occur in various extremes and are highly personalized.

Each student must be individually assessed on how far-reaching this process is for him or her. Our assessment tools sort it out quickly.

Once you know the extent of his or her "whole" versus "individual" processing, you can adapt accordingly. The neuroscientific research on brain processing refers to these converging pathways as the "who" versus the "what." For an individual with extreme right-brain processing, reproducing a "whole" song that he or she just heard is a piece of cake, but analyzing a Bach piece by counting out note-by-note scale degrees in a score is nearly impossible.

For many, this gets diagnosed as a learning disability. The labels include reading-comprehension difficulty, nonverbal learning disorders, ADHD, dyslexia, prosopagnosia, dyscalculia, PDD-NOS, and other varieties. In reality, the individual has no focusing problem; he or she merely has a different approach to the information placed before her. Teaching to the student's style is the key to accelerating his or her learning.

When using "Every Good Boy Does Fine," you target the brain area that assigns meaning to letters—their letters having been assigned to note placement on the staff. This is a three-step translation process that visual learners can do easily. For auditory learners, however, looking and hearing is intuitive, but looking and naming is a great challenge. When first teaching from middle C, higher notes above G are outside of position and are not yet played. Therefore, using the "Every Good Boy Does Fine," model is inappropriate and provides too much information for the task at hand.

When adding finger numbers to the notes, the student will struggle tremendously with translating. To an aural/tactile learner, a finger is a finger. It doesn't need a name. He or she knows it. Even if you travel to a country where you don't speak the language, you'll still have all your limbs. You don't get lost if you can't name your arm in a foreign language. So tap into the strength of the awareness. You can spot an aural learner if he or she completely loses his or her train of thought when you interrupt his or her playing and say, "Oops–use your second finger."

Scales and Rote Learning

In the Rancer Method, scales and rote learning tasks are never introduced. The technic book in the *Alfred Series* introduces only the information that is relative to what the student is learning that week. If for whatever reason you teach these skills to your students, you might notice that the aural learner struggles tremendously to produce with traditional directions for scales. The traditional directions are mind-boggling: Sounds become letters, which become numbers, which become fingers. An aural learner would rather have a root canal without anesthesia than try to decipher this formula:

C-Major Scale Fingering							
	C	D	E	F	G	A	B	C
RH	1	2	3	1	2	3	4	5
LH	5	4	3	2	1	3	2	1

Instead, an ear-based finger system can be incorporated for multi-octave scales:

RH	3 - 4	3 - 4	3 - 4	3 - 4
LH	5 - 3	4 - 3	4 - 3	4 - 3

This table tells the student how many sounds to produce, by ear, in a cluster of three or four. For example, "3" means three sounds, one after the next, in the order of the scale. In a C Major scale, "3" would be "C-D-E". The number "4" means "F-E-D-C". When the next "3" comes around, you start from "C-D-E" in the next octave and continue. This way, with the intention of always starting a new number-cluster with the thumb, the correct fingers will produce the correct pitch in the scale.

This should be practiced with each hand separately. The right hand first produces three sounds. If you begin with the thumb and play three sounds one after the next, you are then available to start over again (with the thumb) to produce the next four sounds. That pattern repeats itself. For the left hand, the sound should always indicate how many sounds are needed, leading back to the thumb. This way, to produce three sounds, one needs to play first with the middle finger and then trace her path back to the thumb. Notice that finger numbers are never mentioned in this lesson. Ear players will organize their fingers automatically to plan on arriving at the end. They can audiate it first, which is why they can recreate it flawlessly.

This tactile approach taps into the ear, and the fingers work with the sound. Students with AP needn't be given charts for each key signature, since they can "hear" the sound and automatically apply the sharps and flats.

If you choose to teach cadences with inversions, know that your AP student can play them by ear in a flash. However, when asked to play inverted cadence from notation, the student will struggle to comprehend what the fuss is about, or why they cannot stick to chords in root position. In the *Alfred Basic Piano Series* used in the Rancer Method, inversions are built into the early learning of chords. By the time the individual has mastered complex playing, he or she has already been developing an appreciation for inversions.

When you teach upper-level theory, ask whether your student can hear the sound by merely looking at the notes. AP aural learners don't always realize that this is so for them; they think everyone does it that way, so you must ask. For them, learning theory on paper is dead information. Rather, play the sound of the information you teach so they can hear how it works. Then the student will comprehend its relevance and get it. Demonstrate the concept without revealing the answers to the theoretical puzzle. Making theory come alive with examples of sound helps the student become proficient in understanding theory. In time, this teaching approach makes them fall in love with theory. Linking the sound to its symbol makes it easy and fun and thus very achievable. Finally, it all comes together.

When writing an academic essay, Henny "hears" the melody of the thought in her head. When the sound dips, she places commas and periods where needed. This process, which is very aural, is similar to how a composer chooses which dynamics to notate into the score. It's also a "whole" process, since the interval of sound can be measured only when heard against the sound of the whole phrase. So too, visual learners look inside the textbook and store the meaning of boldfaced terms, which are the obvious indications to them of which words might appear on the exam. In contrast, the AP auditory student listens during the lecture. When the teacher's voice goes up a major 3rd, that's a pretty good indication that the material is important and will appear on the exam.

To make practical use of this difference, know that it carries over into every area of functioning. For example, the auditory learner will look at a photo of chicken curry, slap together some ingredients, and create something convincingly close. The visual learner will meticulously follow the directions on a box and produce perfect brownies. The synesthete might cook a dish that matches a color/texture association that is pleasing to them. One approach is no more admirable than the other. When a person consistently resorts to one method, it's a sign that he or she leans toward the method that's easiest and fastest for him or her, so he can arrive at the end product as fast as his peers. It's the job of the transformative educator to acknowledge that.

Case Study: Auditory Learner

Case Study 1: A is a ten-year-old autistic boy, the child and grandchild of engineers and mathematicians. To the dismay of his family he struggles tremendously in math. In one session, Susan asked him what 3+6 was, but A was unable to answer. He tried to solve the problem by tapping his fingers on his lap. It was apparent that his brain process kept rebooting halfway through, over and over, and he never got to the finish line. Susan then gave him a set of rhythm sticks, and incorporated Hap Palmer's song *Tap Out the Answer*. Through the song, she sang while questioning, "Three, plus two is?" to which A instantly played out the answer by tapping the sticks together in rhythm to the song. Providing the client a way to demonstrate his intellect is key. If that medium is sound, so be it. In such cases, offer a scribe for exams to write down their answers. How your client arrives at the answer is very individualized, but it's much more pronounced in extreme auditory/tactile learners.

Sensory Issues

Sensory integration dysfunction is very much a part of autism. The perceptual experiences of an autistic person can't be medically measured, since diagnostic tools look for the results of the overload, not how perceptions are magnified within the brain. Underconnectivity in the autistic brain causes a miscommunication of the sensory systems. This overloads the individual systems as each tries to do the job of the four other senses.

Sensory issues are very pronounced in autistic people, and should not be confused with oppositional behavior when the individual responds to a painful overload. Autism is not a behavioral problem. It becomes a behavioral problem only when people don't understand the origin of it as sensory-triggered. When a child reacts to sensory overload, the parent who is observing then reacts to the child's reaction. A sensory overload episode is a trauma each and every time and begs for quiet recuperation time. Early signs of sensory reaction must be addressed. To allow the client to stim is to understand that he has found a tool that works for him, that this particular stim will calm the excessive stimulus so he or she can recharge for whatever comes next.

Never say, "Quiet hands." This is a way of asking the individual to give up something that works to her advantage. That would be equivalent to asking you to pause peeing midstream. You know the relief you feel when the task is complete. So too, these stims are very important for stabilizing input and thereby maximizing brain capacity. Silencing the stims will make your student look like you do without your release.

With sensory integration dysfunction, underconnectivity between the sensory processing areas can cause each of the senses to try its hardest to process what comes at it; however, they cannot pass it along to make sense of it, so it just sits there in that region. This causes overload. Our brain senses work together like a supercomputer. If you close one program, you'll have more memory to run a different one. So too, people with sensory integration can block the visual in order to improve hearing. This is not an acuity issue, as sensory integration doesn't show with standard hearing or vision tests. Often, an autistic person will have 20/20 vision and 100 percent hearing acuity, but might appear unable to hear at all, or see only if he's peering very closely or from the corner of his eyes. For such a person, flapping the hands near the corners of the eyes will instantly overload and shut down the visual processing, and thereby allow the auditory centers to be on high alert. Telling them to "quiet" their hands will make them unable to process the lesson at all. It is the role of the practitioner to redirect the stims so they're more socially acceptable. (See the ideas listed at the end of this section.)

The pons is a very primitive area in the hindbrain. It serves as a relay station carrying signals from various parts of the cerebral cortex to the cerebellum. Nerve impulses coming from the eyes, ears, and touch receptors are sent on to the cerebellum. In the autistic brain, an underdeveloped pons will react to basic situations with a fight-or-flight response. This surge in adrenaline is so common that many individuals describe themselves as being in a constant state of panic. In fight mode, the individual becomes loud, aggressive, obnoxious, screams, is rude, or throws things. In flight mode, the individual will avoid further tasks and procrastinate even in dire emergencies, because nothing else can get in her way until the adrenaline surge dies down. Henny describes her brain as "actively trying to rest," which triggers a vicious cycle of overwork to under-work. A study published in *Frontiers in Neuroinformatics* shows that the brains of autistic children generate an average of 42% more information at rest than do the brains of typically developing children.[11]

---

[11] Velázquez, J. L. P., & Galán, R. F. (2013). Information gain in the brain's resting state: a new perspective on autism. *Frontiers in Neuroinformatics.* 7: 37.

While sensory-integration dysfunction disrupts the communication from one sense to another, each individual area thereby has heightened processing. This explains perfect pitch, the ability to know what ingredients are in a soup just by smelling it, and photographic memory. In a study of Temple Grandin's brain, scans revealed "enhanced white matter in the left inferior fronto-occipital fasciculus, which connects the frontal and occipital lobes and might explain her keen visual abilities."[8]

When NTs (neurotypicals) experience music, they describe the climax as very pleasurable. Autistics have magnified intensity of their processing to the point where the climax triggers an adrenaline rush, which results in both fight and flight responses simultaneously. They want more of it because it's great, but want to run away to avoid the painful sensation engendered by its intensity. In music therapy sessions, if the client is throwing his or her percussion mallets across the room, try to understand what's happening. Most likely, he or she has absolute pitch and even synesthesia. You can see on his or her face that he or she is thoroughly delighted with the music and is enjoying the session, yet he or she throws the mallets across the room. Then he or she gets up to retrieve them and continues drumming. This behavior might repeat itself over and over. The throwing is a mere flight reflex: I want it, but I can't want it, because fight and flight in the musical climax are happening all at once.

Sensory issues cause a physical sensation inside the body, which is a result of the altered perceptions. Many individuals get dizzy or nauseated, as they have a vestibular reaction to visual and sound distortions. Others exhibit fatigue and depletion of their cognitive strengths after significant exposure. Stimming is Mother Nature's brilliant tool for rewiring the brain for better functioning and for coping with imbalanced sensations and emotions. Self-stimulatory behaviors are necessary since both anxiety and joy will trigger imbalance. Any out of-the-ordinary or unplanned stimulus becomes an unscripted occurrence. Since it is under-equipped to process this, the brain goes on high alert and the individual panics, which demands a calming technique.

In the body, sensory anxiety feels like air bubbles in the joints. For those bubbles to disperse, an urge to "sneeze" them out arises. Hand flapping, wrist flicking, and twitching are all very effective. It's entirely possible for autistic people to be unaware of the connection between stimming and the relief it brings. Indeed, the flapping seems to appear as if it were a spontaneous burst of neural activity, like a tic. The brilliance of these stims is that, aside from the sensory relief, they also serve as a cognitive rewiring for processing information.

If you had to sit at your desk to do homework and your table was a giant mess, you'd likely be unable to find a clear spot to do your work. You might develop an urge to reshuffle the messy pile and clear a spot, and after you have, you might find yourself sighing with relief. Your whole body feels better just from visually taking in the neatness. A clean desk is a sign of a clear mind, as the mind aches for clarity.

With the limitations of an underdeveloped processing center in the brain, more brain power is needed to process even the basics. If there are sensory-integration issues, then more than one sense can't be effectively processed simultaneously. The world around us is a multisensory environment; thus the cumulative barrage is intense and constant. The type of stim observed can be indicative of a sensory irritation or a sensory need. Some individuals have a need to touch and smear and scoop and squeeze. Yet others have a terrifying aversion to textures and sounds. The stimming is a signal of what's going on inside. Whether the individual is sensory defensive or seeking, both result from the brain inefficiently processing the input, i.e., processing too much or too little of it.

The small area between the fingers, where they meet the rest of the hand, can be especially sensitive. This is because in that area the two fingers are most likely to touch each other all the time, and skin-to-skin contact can be quite painful for the underdeveloped pons. Skin feels like a whisper, a subtle breeze; it's neither entirely here nor there. This textural inconsistency makes it a gray area for the brain, which processes all or none of it. Since the fingers are a part of the person and are always touching, the contact is constant. There's little escape from this kind of torment. Every now and then, a good shake of the hand or twitching of the fingers will help dissolve the sensation. On a magnified level, clapping the hands causes more skin-to-skin contact. Wearing clothes that don't cover the most skin possible, such as summer shorts, can also overload. Hugs are of course the epitome of overload for this very reason.

Visual processing differences can also present as a convergence insufficiency. It's important to understand that despite 20/20 vision, this can manifest itself as (1) double vision; (2) bouncing of words on the page; (3) constant crossing of the two pictures from the double vision; (4) each eye seeing a discrete picture as if through separate toilet-paper tubes. The brain must then try to put those two pictures together. As it works to do that, the images repeatedly move together and then snap apart. Given these exhausting challenges, visual overload is nearly constant.

The subtle flickering of a fluorescent light overhead (invisible to people with typical processing) causes a strobe effect that would lead to seizures in those with seizure disorders. Here, the lights begin to cause overload through headache, nausea, pain behind the eyes, and fatigue. A visual stim solves that problem. When weakening the eye muscles so that the vision is blurred, the brain "reboots" and becomes more receptive to the next chunk of input. To an observer, this stim looks like the individual is staring at nothing, eyes glazed. That might be misinterpreted as disinterest, lost focus, or even "Wow, she's making eye contact." Inside, though, all is calm. For people who wear glasses, removing them can instantly provide a calming, blurry bliss.

Irlen lenses (Irlen.com,) prisms, or custom tints can also help calm the input, so that overload occurs only after more input, extending the processing time. Though the media have condemned visual training exercises and Irlen lenses as controversial, it's important to note that affected individuals find tremendous relief in these treatments. Unlike special diets and vitamin regimens, they can provide a simple fix despite the lack of extensive research supporting the methods.

Vocal stims are effective and portable, albeit not very private. If the individual is walking on a street where there's an overhead train, he or she can hum a loud monotone in her head, so that the sound, vibrating inside, overshadows the train's sounds. Also, constricting the breathing in a slightly nasal manner makes the sound of the air passing through the nose audible from the inside. These soft sounds offer the white noise that serves the same purpose of "rebooting" without having to cover one's ears.

The art of stimming is to neutralize sensory stimuli that can lead to overload. If a person can't create these essential tools for himself on demand, he'll be constantly overwhelmed, which leads to furious stimming in an attempt to equalize again. Spinning or rocking is a result of extreme overload, and the hope behind the movement is to create some physical force to shift the internal pressure. Social situations too can trigger the brain into overload, and stimming helps alleviate that pain. Misunderstanding social interaction or communication intentions and not processing lights can all lead to overload, since underconnectivity is the cause of all these issues.

Please do not force any individual to stop stimming. It's a survival tool and very necessary. If a stim is inappropriate for public display, please learn to read a student's signs and develop a newer, more appropriate stim that works. For students who tug on their shirt collars, try introducing a soft scarf with fringes, which can be worn every day. For students who bite their knuckles, try introducing a large wooden beaded necklace or belt. Shoe inserts that have tactile markings can lessen the urge to jump and run. Koosh key chains can be a lifesaver, and 1.5-inch hedge balls that look like porcupines can be kept in hoodie pockets for privacy. While one hand is in the pocket, filling its needs with a hedge ball, the rest of the brain is available to plow through assignments at record speed.

Constantly moving the fingers helps a person think, which is why playing the piano provides such a healthy neural workout. The clinician should help develop a conscious understanding of the urges in public, so that hands can be restrained (by choice) inside the pockets, where there should always be a tiny fidget toy.

Rewarding someone for not flapping is like rewarding someone for not wincing when he puts his hand on a hot waffle iron. The "quiet hands" or "sitting on hands" approach to behavior modification is unacceptable. Instead, the environment should be altered so as not to trigger the individual into reacting.

Misunderstood Stimming

Sensory Integration Disorder was excluded from The Diagnostic and Statistical Manual of Mental Disorders (DSM-5) despite the issues being a substantial part of an Autism Spectrum Disorder (ASD). ABA (Applied Behavior Analysis) is based on Pavlov's operant conditioning for dogs and is entirely inappropriate for managing human behavior that is assumed to be problematic.

When you have a headache, what do you do? Take Tylenol? Take a shower? Go crazy? Get snappy? Imagine the brilliance of autism, wherein Mother Nature helps individuals cope with enormous sensory pain 24/7: Flapping is Tylenol; vocal stims are Motrin; lining up objects is Aspirin; and reciting facts is codeine. Tylenol helps with bone pain, and flapping your limbs will relieve that. Motrin is an anti-inflammatory, and is wonderful with relieving muscle pain.

Vocal stims overload the auditory system so that tactic pain is not ignored or overlooked by the response system. Aspirin works as a blood-thinner and dilates your blood vessels, thus improving blood flow. Lining up objects reorganizes chaos or traffic in the brain pathways needed for accessing other areas. Codeine is a narcotic which numbs out nerve endings and allows us to not feel much. Reciting facts takes over the control of the immediate task at hand (reciting from memory) so that everything else is shut out. (Note: Do not use these medications as a replacement for these stims. This is merely an analogy, and not medical advice.) These purely sensory behaviors are widely misinterpreted, mainly for lack of information. This section aims to change the protocol of thinking by association, which labels stimming as a "behavior problem."

Stimming is Mother Nature's brilliant tool for rewiring the brain for better functioning and coping with imbalanced sensations and emotions. Self-stimulatory behaviors are necessary, since both anxiety and joy will trigger an imbalance. Henny has learned how to deal with any out of-the-ordinary, unplanned and unscripted occurrences. First comes the unavoidable panic, triggered by the brain's inability to cope, which is the same as the adrenaline fight/flight response in a fearsome situation.

We cannot emphasize this analogy enough. In the body, sensory/anxiety feels like air bubbles in the joints. In order for those air bubbles to disseminate, there rises an urge to "sneeze" them out. Hand flapping, wrist-flicking or twitching are very effective. It is entirely possible for autistic individuals not to be aware of the connection between stimming and the relief it brings. Indeed, the flapping seems to appear as if it were a spontaneous burst of neural activity, like a tic. Aside from the sensory relief, it also serves as a cognitive rewiring for processing information. That's why we call it Mother Nature's brilliant tool for coping.

In her book *Thinking In Systems*, Donella H. Meadows writes:

> A complex system with balancing feedback loops … is your ability to sweat and shiver to maintain your body temperature … their presence is critical to the long-term welfare of the system. One of the big mistakes we make is to strip away these "emergency" response mechanisms because they aren't often used and they appear to be costly. In the short term, we see no effect from doing this. In the long-term, we drastically narrow the range of conditions over which the system can survive. One of the heartbreaking ways we do this is in encroaching on the habitats of endangered species. Another is in the encroaching on our own time for personal rest, recreation, socialization, and medication (p. 153).[12]

To advance this logic, Meadows says:

---

[12] Meadows, D. H. (2008), *Thinking in systems: A primer* (White River Junction, VT: Chelsea Green Publishing Company), pg. 156.

> Strengthening balancing feedback controls improve a system's self-correcting abilities ... [such as] preventative medicine, exercise, and good nutrition to bolster the body's ability to fight disease (p. 154).

A balancing feedback loop is self-correcting; a reinforcing feedback loop is self-reinforcing. The more it works, the more it gains power to work some more, driving system behavior in one direction (p. 155). Stimming serves as a self-correcting balancing feedback loop to gain power for driving the sensory system in one direction.

> The ability to self-organize is the strongest form of system resilience. A system that can evolve can survive almost any change, by changing itself (p. 159).

Susan's first introduction to Henny's insight into the subject came during Henny's visit to Susan's home studio. By observing the students in Susan's private practice, Henny was able to link their individual stimming to actual environmental stimuli. By accommodating and modifying minor details in the studio, all the issues the students were struggling with disappeared. Dimming specific lights had an almost analgesic effect on one student. Switching from broken chords to softer *legato* accompaniment enabled one very distressed student to uncover his ears for the first time in the session.

Additional accommodations targeted specific integration needs. When learning piano, several of the senses are needed to work together in order for the student to produce sound. First, he or she must visually process the notes on the page, and we hope his or her eyes are tracking across the page with sufficient convergence. Then, she must have a sensorimotor response to the notes, which makes the correct finger press the correct key. For a student with absolute pitch, this process is interrupted when she looks at the note and hears its sound in her head. A beginner at music lessons will struggle to push through to the next step. If a sensorimotor response occurs and he plays the key, then he no longer retains the visual memory and loses his place on the page.

To streamline sensory integration, positive sensory input is needed. If the individual wishes to self-stimulate his sensory system, he will flap, bounce, twiddle, or shift in his seat. By overloading the kinesthetic input, the other system can reboot and be on duty. To point to the music is not always enough help for students to stay put and not lose their place on the page. Some students have benefited from a soft bristled plastic grassy bath mat placed on the floor near the piano pedals. The students who appreciate this positive sensory input will enter the room and immediately strip off their shoes and socks with delight.

Students have also learned to make requests for weighted items for positive-pressure input. When incorporating a weighted lap pad, all calm takes over. Make sure to drape the pad over the knees so that the pressure expresses the "air bubbles." The joints are begging for it. In the instance of younger children who have a hard time falling asleep, their restlessness could appear to be anxiety. It might help to use a weighted blanket or a pressure massage of the joints.

Empowerment and dignifying people's abilities, i.e., teaching to the gift, helps accomplish a quality of life for all humans. Teaching to the weaknesses is a standard of practice for billing insurance companies, but there's no room for it in strength-based modalities. The only truly disabling condition is the human one. It's the expectations of the people around us that make us seem wrong.

Synesthesia

> *People who "see with white ears, hear with their eyes".*
> *—David Tubergen, PhD*

This quote is intended to be a head scratcher for the majority who cannot fathom such experiences. Synesthesia is a brain phenomenon that creates multi-sensory perceptions in which the senses are crossed. Some synesthetic individuals associate certain letters with colors, and others do that with numbers. For example, Henny sees an F minor chord as a beautiful shade of light blue. Susan's husband, Mike, sees the number six as bluish-white. No two persons with synesthesia see the same colors or shapes for the same data, because what they see is unique to how their brains perceive the input. Some synesthetes will tell you that the sound of their name is a dynamic shade of red. Others say that when they're balancing their checkbook, the totals are a pretty purple. To others, a specific word will make them hear a sound, or taste a texture.

> *I was fifteen before I realized most people don't have colored hearing.*
> —Shimra Starr
>
> *When a bowling ball hits the pins, the sound is also a word. A nonsense word, but a word nonetheless.*
> —Mike Rancer
>
> *When I see green fireworks, I hear the name of a person that I know. Their name in turn gives me this texture and color on my tongue*
> —Henny Kupferstein

Musicians might not be aware of their synesthesia. They're the people who see musical notes dancing in their line of vision. They can notate anything they just heard in real time. Because of the taboo surrounding mental illness and hallucinations, few people would share that they see these shapes or colors. No one wants to be labeled as seeing or hearing what others don't.

The word "illusion" comes from the Latin *illusio,* defined as mocking or deceit. Modern dictionaries define illusion as an erroneous perception of reality. Typically, people determine their reality by seeing, hearing, tasting, smelling, and touching—the five senses that help tell us what's going on around us. How accurately do our senses report back whether what we see or hear is really what others do?

It's the job of our conscious mind to sort out these stimuli and make some sense of them for us. Synesthesia, however, is purely a subconscious perception. It can't be suppressed, and neither can you will yourself into that state. People who experiment with psychedelic drugs might experience an awareness of synesthesia. Dr. Oliver Sacks describes his vivid perceptions in his book *Hallucinations*.

When you look at an optical illusion, you feel a bit out of sorts. You know you're looking at lines and dots, yet you see an image jumping, dancing, moving, and blending together. These illusions are designed to trick your mind into questioning its objective interpretation of reality. For people with synesthesia, their reality is not theirs to interpret. Their senses are crossed, and the information just appears, but the more they think about it, the sooner they lose it. An AP'er stores the pitch memory, while a synesthete stores the qualitative memory of the whole sound. Speech or left-brained logic will dismantle that whole memory. Once you break it apart to analyze it, you lose the whole picture.

This is how savants reproduce music. They hear it, sense it, and reproduce it. If you asked them to analyze the melody and tell you what key it's in, they wouldn't be able to tell you without thinking. After all that thought, they might lose their original perceptions of the melody, and reproduce only a technical breakdown of it without color or emotion. Earlier, we explained how calendar-calculator savants use right-brain subconscious perceptions to give you their answers, rather than engage the left brain to compute rapidly. This information is held between the synaptic clefts, where inspiration and insight make their appearance, as if "out of the blue." They appear as whole gestalt. These are the cohesive, coherent impressions that engender creative clarity.

Educators, clinicians, parents, and music therapists must never silence the vocalization of these perceptions. Provide a safe place for the individual to express how she sees things. These perceptions are very powerful; they take center stage, and cannot be shut out. As Henny describes synesthesia: "If you wake up every single day and the whole world around you says, "The sky is green," how long till you go crazy?"

People with synesthesia can use music to express their perceptions. These are the pieces that listening to makes your heart stop. You can hear, see, and taste the emotion; you can literally feel your skin crawling in a sensory way. That's a positive outcome of synesthesia, but we need to respect the journey required for this ability to arrive there. For many, turning these perceptions into music is very easy, and provides an outlet for venting these "wild visions" into a medium revered by the masses. By introducing music theory and composition to such individuals, you offer a priceless gift of empowerment.

A synesthetic student sits in class and hears everything differently from everyone else there. This is the student who'll disagree with your idea about a major triad sounding happy and a minor triad sad. She isn't trying to be rude, disrespectful, or obnoxious. For Henny, jumping back and forth between major and minor sounds like switching back and forth between shoes and sneakers. It also feels like the difference between the cold, hard sharpness of all the cracks in the pavement and the warm, soft support that cushions it.

While these expressions are dramatically outside the norm, they should still be respected. They come from an entirely subconscious place and are not malicious. A student who's silenced will be made to feel like he's crazy. This goes back to the "sky is green" analogy. We don't want to suppress this ability; we want to provide a safe haven for it. Nurtured, it will develop into something larger than life for the benefit of all. Those who don't have synesthesia would be well advised to seek ways of analyzing unusual art and begin mapping a new reality for themselves.

In musicians, first observe for clues that the person is processing music in a kinesthetic manner. In addition to AP traits, some of these traits are parallel with AP'ers as well:

- They are excellent writers.
- They possess a keen sense of directionality.
- They move to the music in unusual ways.

Accommodating The Individual Gift 157

- When singing, they will shake in an atypical manner, such as on the subdivision or on the offbeat.
- They will roll their eyes in an orgasmic way when the music climaxes.
- They respond most to songs in a certain key, because that specific key "feels right" to them.
- They compose very colorful music.
- They might see the pain when others are feeling hurt.
- They will see blood and feel it in their bodies.
- If they relied on synesthetic perceptions to learn/retain information all their lives, they might struggle tremendously to make sense of stimuli if they lose their synesthesia through a traumatic brain injury or if it fades later in life.
- Audiating a number or word in their heads produces a vision or color rather than their seeing the number or word printed on page.
- They might solve a math problem by seeing the total as a color.
- Some sounds will trigger a taste or texture in their mouths, and the individual might avoid playing music in a certain key.
- They have a strong memory for intervallic data such as calculation totals and computation of numbers.
- They remember people's names as a "fact," and can tell you where they met that person, and what they were eating then (smell), but might not be able to attach the name to a person's face.
- They might be thought of as insane, or might be misdiagnosed with a mental illness such as schizophrenia.
- A person with sound-color synesthesia might be naturally drawn to someone with a pretty voice, while avoiding those whose voices are "sharp" or "glaring."

Autistic students with magnified synesthesia might throw their mallets across the room while playing. This is an involuntary fight/flight adrenaline reaction to the sensations they feel when the music intensifies. It's not a behavioral issue, since they usually get up and retrieve the mallets and continue playing. This might happen the moment a drum rhythm hits a steady groove. Bringing the groove down to more of a "monotone" will trigger fewer synesthetic perceptions for such a client, ensuring a flow throughout the session. Also, when playing, the client should be advised to "put less emotion into the music" so as not to overload on sensations that will interrupt the music making. This is an extreme situation, and the client's reaction to sound should be monitored to ensure that this is indeed the cause.

Henny says that for repeated practice before a performance, she had to emotionally disconnect in order to get through it each time, because "it kept stabbing me."

It's also important to understand and validate the person with synesthesia. Because the inner perception is instant and so stark, it doesn't occur to the synesthete that this is not reality for other people. David Tubergen is a seventy-year-old concert violinist and a true virtuoso. He was Susan's violin teacher in college. In a recent conversation about his life with absolute pitch, Susan asked him about his reading comprehension. He soon recounted his struggles with math, reading comprehension, and even sight-reading. Despite earning a full scholarship to NYU and Yale, he came away with a PhD only because of his musical talents and fabulous writing skills.

When Susan asked him, "What color is the number three?" he said yellow. He said the letter G was blue. Susan then revealed to him that he had synesthesia. Dr. Tubergen didn't know what it was, and was floored that no one had ever cared about it before. People with absolute pitch and synesthesia are easily spotted by observation of their behaviors. In academia, these are the most colorful writers. Henny's writing gives the reader a multisensory experience; her words make every sentence palpable.

On the subject of validating a person's inner perceptions, let's talk about Susan's husband, Mike, and daughter Emily. Mike and Emily are very much a left-brain father-and-daughter pair. Mike worked in budgeting his whole life, and Emily earned a degree in journalism followed by a master's in business administration. Both have synesthesia with words and numbers. This ability is purely perceptual, since both see different colors for the same data. They're a perfect example of a balanced brain that can use left-brain logic while tapping into the perceptual benefits of right-brain processes. Emily has absolute pitch, and Susan never understood why she was entirely uninterested in studying music. Susan started Emily on piano at a young age, but Emily soon quit. In middle school, she was accidentally put in choir for a short time, but she couldn't wait to get out of it. She does, however, continue to love listening to music.

When Susan began to research the differences between the left- and right-brain variations of absolute pitch, Emily's traits lined up instantly. Emily is also an artist, which could confuse the person assessing such an individual. One might jump to the conclusion that an artist is a right-brainer, but on further questioning, Emily said that she loves to draw pictures from magazines, capturing the lines, shadows, and structure of the photo. Emily also hates to be faced with a blank canvas. She craves the design of a system, which she follows spectacularly. When she was the editor of a newspaper, she was responsible for laying out the text, ads, and photos into the framework of the template. Such is the nature of the highly visual learner. When you throw absolute pitch into the mix, you find that the person merely replicates the systems placed before her, as she excels in sight-reading, but when given a blank canvas and asked to improvise or compose, she just doesn't know where to start.

Susan had quite an eye-opening evening when she, Mike, Emily, and Henny went out together. Over dinner, synesthesia was discussed. Suddenly, Mike was adamant about the number six being blueish-white, and Henny was putting her foot down about F# being light blue. Emily was describing how she looks at charts and sees the totals in a color representing a numerical value. This color does not match up as a combination of the numbers totaled. For Mike, spreadsheets are easy as pie. Mike is studying Spanish, and as much as he wants to gain fluency, he has difficulty acquiring the language strictly auditorily, and must have the visual. Emily picked up French auditorily and adapted to the accent by "listening to the tone", largely due to her AP.

Susan felt completely out of place throughout the entire discussion. For the first time in her life, she had the fleeting experience of what it would be like if she didn't have a brain phenomenon but had to be in the presence of many who do. Rather than being enthralled with the discussion, she drifted into a distant zone, waiting for the "weirdoes" to finish talking. At one point, the waiter came by and Henny said, "This is it, we'll settle this now. Sir, the number six isn't blue, right?" The poor man fled to the safety of the other tables, where people were seeing food rather than numbers. It was quite comical.

There's a fine line between turning such persons into a parlor trick and validating their differences. Without any recognition, they won't know that they have an exquisite gift that others don't have. Certainly, they are a talented bunch, and many famous artists and composers have been known to possess it. Since they can see things more vividly, they have an advantage over everyone else. That needs to be tapped into. Encourage such individuals to keep a journal, to keep writing, and keep composing music. Since they have such extraordinary abilities, you need to be able to ask the right questions, so they realize that they have a gift and that you can unwrap it. They will look at you in a special way because you pointed it out. Suddenly, you're the one who's important, because you're the one who figured it out. Similarly, if you figure out what's going on with a perfect pitcher, you become the person who first considered the gift and turbocharged the journey of self-exploration.

For those with synesthesia, the senses are over-connected, causing a crossing of the senses. Overload occurs when the stimulus perceived by the brain is different from typical sensory perceptions. If the person has synesthesia, she will have a crossing of the senses. This means that while each sense is trying to process what it just took in, it's also processing the stimulus from the other regions—at the same time. So your tongue tries to hear and your eyes try to listen. This too can lead to rapid overload. Auditory learners are grossly misunderstood. Contrary to broad stereotypes, auditory learners are not a minority. Over 400 individuals whom we randomly surveyed described a long history of being misunderstood, which lead to a pattern of specific life paths. Not understanding the auditory learning style is why many such learners flunk out of excellent programs in universities from which they secured prestigious scholarships. This is also why auditory learners abandon the study of music at some point in their lives. In many cases, they've simply started to believe that they are just plain stupid or learning disabled.

A successful educational relationship occurs when neurodiversity is incorporated into the program design. The best educators are those who have experience blending multimodal processes into a system that's been shown to work for all types of students. Often, a learning disability is diagnosed when a student fails to learn in an environment that is rigid and not accommodating to her needs. In college, a professor told Henny, "If you can't prove to me that you're thinking it through the way I taught the class to think it through, then it means you don't understand it." Sadly, this educator revealed how unable he was to think outside of his own style.

Hyperlexia, Dyscalculia, Prosopagnosia, and Photographic Memory

Hyperlexia is an inexplicable ability to read at a very young age without having been formally taught. *Dyscalculia* is a mathematics disability stemming from the inability to compute or process anything numerical. *Photographic memory* stems from eidetic memory abilities, which can be visual and auditory. *Prosopagnosia* is an inability to distinguish one person's face from another, also called face-blindness.

These curious phenomena are often bundled with an autism diagnosis; however, each comes with its own curious abilities. Instead of taking the time to list weaknesses, it's important to review how they contribute to a very unusual and strong group of skill sets. Such individuals, "eidetikers," have remarkable abilities. Remembering everything you've ever heard or seen can be very overloading. The teacher's essential job is to carve these memories into functional skills that apply to growth development.

Identifying these skills in a student begins with observing his or her approach to music. Does it seem like he or she is playing without thinking? If he or she is playing back anything he just heard, then there's a chance that he isn't processing the fundamentals at all. Rather, he can play it back from memory and not from conceptual organization. The role for the educator begins when you remove the tool for expressing the playback. For example, can a chess player recount an entire game without having any pieces to demonstrate the steps for you? If so, that's perfect recall. Alan Searleman, a professor of psychology at St. Lawrence University in New York, says, "If eidetic imagery were truly 'photographic' in nature, you wouldn't expect any errors at all."

If your student displays such exceptionality in music, honor it. Also understand that such a student might be using a lot of right-brain memory to perform. In that case, left-brain encoding never occurs. These are students who struggle greatly to learn math concepts. When you ask the parent or teacher, "How is she in math?" you might get mixed responses. This is because a student might be able to answer tenth-grade algebra questions without showing her work process. This student might also be sitting in her third-grade Special Ed classroom unable to understand how two blocks and one block add up to the number three.

Fundamental concepts for learning are vital to the majority of the student population in schools today, but when students with such specific brain makeup enter the school system, a hostile learning environment assaults their way of thinking. Every weakness explodes in their face, and strength-based learning falls to the wayside. Typically developed eidetikers begin to lose the ability after age six as they learn to process information more abstractly. If, however, abstract concepts elude the complexly wired brain, then the memory remains the only way to master new material. By teaching to the student's strengths, and adding layers of complexity as the lessons progress, new neural pathways are formed.

Visual aids used in the classroom can prevent the auditory thinker from learning. Rather, building new pathways to left-brain functions opens up the brain to additional cognitive tools. This is a crucial first step in abstract computation for formal models of scientific thinking. The autistic and complex brain already has access to permanent memory. This is the *gestalt* form of learning, which can be superb for specific areas of production; however, to develop the finer details of analytical thinking, additional pathways must be built.

In music lessons, no better way exists than teaching piano. The auditory learner begins making sounds right away. Five new letters of the musical vocabulary are introduced immediately when the student plays real songs with letters from C to G. The piano is an instrument which is linear, and sounds going up or down in steps makes so much sense. This aural introduction to patterned-thinking stimulates the brain to think abstractly across multiple senses. The piano is the most appropriate way to introduce musicianship, which is a language that translates to every instrument thereafter.

The use of circle drawings to teach math concepts is as foreign to such a student as is the introduction of musical notation in the first lesson. The standard of piano pedagogy is to begin introducing notation starting from middle C. That means that the student sometimes leaves the lesson playing C and D over and over again. In math class, that's the same as seeing those two blocks over and over again and understanding neither the meaning of the blocks in the math problem nor the dots on the page of musical notation.

Such students might be exceptional at solving high-level algebraic equations. Try them! Rather than have them spend three years in Special Education puzzling over circle games, try presenting real math problems several grade levels higher. Similarly, in the music lesson, teach to the strength. Starting with the Rancer Method gets the individual to produce immediately and intelligently. As they continue with the lessons, left-brain abilities begin to emerge. This is true with every student Susan and Henny have observed.

Chapter Eight

How Do Savants Do It?

How do savants do it?

They don't.

Most savants have absolute pitch, regardless of whether they're calendar-calculator, musical savants, or artistic savants.[13] This means that they can be of the right- or left-brain variation and still have absolute pitch. For right-brained perfect pitchers (RBAPs), no thinking is involved. They don't process (left-brain), they perceive (right-brain). Of course, there are overlapping variations, and people have benefited from new pathways bridged due to exercises and therapies. Here we continue to describe the right-brained variation of a savant with absolute pitch.

If you ask a right-brainer to think about a pitch, she is unable to answer. If she tries to think about it extensively, she often gets lost halfway through. So too, savant abilities originate by default perception rather than high-speed left-brain logic. Neurotypicals need to take drugs to experience multi sensory perceptions; savants experience them since conception.

---

[13] Treffert, Darold A., *Extraordinary People: Understanding Savant Syndrome* (New York: Harper & Row, 1989).

Splinter Skills

Can we all develop savant skills? That's what Dr. Treffert writes in his book *Islands of Genius*. Autistic students often get in trouble with the school district, and are failed in math class even if they're calendar-calculator savants. What exactly does this mean? The person is able to write the answers to all the math problems, but is unable to show his or her work process. To a typical educator, if you can't show how you computed the answer, then the answer is no longer important. To the extreme right-brained person with savant-level perceptions, these answers are multisensory perceptions that simply present themselves visually or through taste, smell, or touch. For example, when Henny is in the supermarket, she can look at the shopping cart and tell you to the last cent how much your total will be; however, she struggles so much with math that she'll get lost halfway through when trying to count her own fingers. This is a fine example of a splinter skill.

So what's happening here? The answer "$82.43" is simply there; it suddenly just appears in Henny's head. Her body sees it, tastes it, and feels it all at once. There's a complete inability to explain it or break it down into a formula, as she is unable to consciously add up the prices of everything in the cart. No logic was used to compute that total. It was a mere perceptual process.

Musical savants are able to hear something and play it back for you. When Henny first began to do that on piano, she was unable to say what key the song was in, what style of song it was, or on which scale degree it began. To the untrained musician, those are breakdowns of a fact that already occurred. For Henny, the brain produces the end result. The logical process never happened.

Savants appear to be using extreme left-brain logic to come up with math answers, but are still not considered left-brain individuals. This is because they're not using the conscious left brain to compute in a formulaic manner. Indeed, savants struggle to explain how they got to their answers. They can give you the product, but not the process. This is because they don't actually compute or process at all. This in no way implies that theirs isn't an intelligent production.

Savant abilities are inexplicable skills with an extreme level of proficiency, where that level of mastery is achieved in typical people only after very lengthy training. We've heard the stories of the man who woke up after a seizure and was able to play piano on a prodigious level. You might also know a calendar-calculator savant in your community. Perhaps you or your child has been able to play an instrument since birth, without having ever studied it. These abilities can be explained now. (Prodigies and savants are not the same thing; the differences are explained in chapter 2).

The key to explaining "inexplicable savant abilities" and young prodigies is to first understand the origin of the ability. Dr. Treffert refers to this as "genetic memory," since it is there by nature rather than nurture. The gift is primal and raw and purely an ability immediately available without thinking. When you introduce the thinking, savants feel like floundering fools because they can't answer your question. This is because the answers appear as a "whole" in the synapses, more like a *gestalt* perception than a traceable pattern of thought based on fundamental building blocks and *figure-ground* extraction.

Henny is an extreme right-brained patterned thinker and has absolute pitch. She can see massive amounts of random information and can connect the dots instantly. In music, her fingers are tapping the melodies in real time while listening to them. Henny can notate an entire ensemble she's just heard, but cannot notate only one part. Because of the way her brain is wired, she's unable to extract a single stream of sound from a greater whole. That would require sensory integration, i.e., the five senses communicating with each other. Instead of growing those pathways, Henny has more intense abilities within each of her five senses, but only when they're isolated. If music is playing in the background, she cannot do any homework, and if a song with words is playing or a radio announcer is talking, she becomes unable to read or write until the sound of the words is done. Susan cannot focus when music is playing. This is because she is consciously analyzing without wanting to, which dominates all her available working memory and creates a distraction from the task at hand.

Dr. Bong Walsh, a neuroscientist from the San Francisco Bay Area, emailed Henny:

> I was always extraordinarily far ahead of my peers with math & numbers, but I was one of those kids who never knew how to show his work. What exactly was I supposed to show? I just knew the answer, virtually instantaneously. This frustrated many a teacher and made many others marvel. I so often got asked: But *how* do you know? How did you figure it out? And then I'd have to try to figure out how I figured it out, and this was always the toughest task by far.

Dr. Walsh has a very high level of absolute pitch, and was able to note-name from recorded pitches on a CD, as tested by Susan in 2013.

Alpha Waves and Right-Brain Perceptual Processing

Regarding conscious processing and subconscious perceptions, Dr. Joaquin Farias is a very colorful researcher from Spain. Henny attended one of his lectures on neuroplasticity in 2012. In a diagram of the brain's electroencephalograph (EEG) patterns, he pointed to alpha waves, which are the peak moments for superlearning. In an EEG, patterns are classified into two types of waves, beta and alpha. Beta waves are those associated with day-to-day wakefulness.

During periods of relaxation while awake, our brain waves become slower, increase in amplitude, and become more synchronous. These are called alpha waves, often associated with states of relaxation and peacefulness during meditation and biofeedback. Dr. Farias called this the present of the subconscious. Through our constant judging, our conscious mind always focuses on the past and the future, but we also have a vast amount of unconscious thinking going on that applies to the present state, and we should use it for superlearning.

In order to bring about this hypnoidal state for greatest learning, Farias showed the audience an exercise that involved pointing a finger in the air and then turning it clockwise, very slowly, while the hand and arm was stationary. This was then repeated in counterclockwise motion. The same was done with another finger on the hand. The key for this to work was the eye fixation, as you had to focus on a spot and not look away. After about two minutes, Farias announced that we are ready to retain information. Indeed, the audience members felt refreshed and ready to drink it all in.

Focal dystonia is a neurological condition that Dr. Farias treats in his private practice. He admits that he most often treats musicians and surgeons. His explanation for this phenomenon involves a body-image-refresh of the brain function. Apparently, the brain snaps about 300 images of our body every second. Within twenty-four hours, a new image is formed, so if you had a cast on your leg for six weeks, you'd be unable to move the leg well enough to walk immediately after the cast was removed. Ironically, this is not because of the leg being motionless for so long, but because by snapping those images, the brain taught itself, "Oh, this part shall remain motionless." In order for the brain to know the latest update, we must begin moving the leg by intervention such as physical therapy. Those movements will show the brain the new image.

When an individual plays a musical instrument incessantly, often for practice, the body recognizes the finger placements as "Oh, that's where it belongs." Focal dystonia can occur when that finger refuses to move in any other way. The syndrome is a poorly understood condition that often affects musicians. Also found in writers, it's commonly referred to as writer's cramp or graphospasm. Symptoms usually occur when trying to do a task that requires repetitive fine motor movements, such as practicing music for hours on end. Because of the cramping and discomfort upon onset, this is often misdiagnosed as carpal tunnel syndrome.

Dr. Farias knows how to treat focal dystonia. In the reversal process, the client is asked to do specific repetitive movements to enter a trancelike hypnoidal state evidenced by alpha waves on an EEG. In this short-lived state of mind, the ability to receive and retain information can be permanent. In this induced state, the fingers are straightened, and new learned behavior for the correct stress-free hand movements can be taught and retained. In this hypnoidal state, the brain captures new images of its body and stores the message "Oh, this is how it belongs." As the person slips out of the hypnoidal state, a new permanent body image is retained.

The doctor's lecture was targeted to music students who wished to learn how best to use their practice time. By recognizing that we all have moments when our alpha waves peak, we are taught to step away when the learning seems to not be happening. When a person enters the superlearning hypnoidal mode, learning the music is permanent. One should therefore follow a hypnoidal state with a sleep state rather than practice obsessively. These are some very important findings that every musician should know and try to follow.

It is also during this potent high alpha state when neuroplastic changes occur to trigger visual motor cohesion in people with dyspraxia (difficulty with motor planning and movement, comorbid in autism). For right-brain absolute pitchers, especially those with synesthesia, the answers present themselves aurally in the subconscious hypnoidal state where multisensory perceptions are formed. This is not a perception one can suppress, nor can anyone will him or herself into using it. As a result, musical savants can play anything they hear, but can't tell you in what key they're playing in. As soon as they try to use logic, they lose the sensory perception. This is more pronounced in the autistic population wherein sensory integration challenges halt thought when one tries to engage more than one sense at a time.

The difference between savants and giftedness is determined by whether the left brain is engaged or not. If the right brain is used exclusively to perceive answers, it's a savant ability. If the left brain is engaged to think it through formulaically, it's giftedness. That individual has a conscious ability to engage his left brain to compute, but does it very well, resulting in a high level of ability. The goal of the Rancer Method is to stimulate left-brain thinking for extreme right-brain absolute-pitch possessors. For those who have benefited from this method, dramatic changes in reading comprehension and mathematics skills have been noted. The goal is to use this method for more than 30 percent of one's lifetime to derive the greatest benefit. In the average 4 year-old student, the benefits are obvious after 20 months of training (30% of their lifetime).

Hundreds of individuals have been surveyed and observed for these benefits, and many are highlighted as a success story. Individuals who've been sight-reading for more than 30 percent of their lifetimes have been able to benefit from access to the left-brain functions necessary for abstract thinking (we call them "the LBAP/RBAP morphs"). These functions are vital for computational ability and logic building for mathematics and reading comprehension.

Chapter Nine

Autism and Sensory Integration

Three people are seated in a doctor's office. One has cerebral palsy, the second has had a leg amputated, and the third had a stroke just last year. What do they all have in common? All three appear to have limited or no use of the left leg. By having all three present, the doctor can determine whether the reasons for their challenges are physical, such as the leg being absent, or neurological, such as brain damage to the area responsible for that limb. Sometimes there is a blood disorder causing the muscles not to contract and relax as needed. To the naked eye though, all three appear to have the same "problem."

This book bridges three worlds together for your understanding. Among the authors, we have autism, sensory integration issues and absolute pitch. By combining our experiences, we can learn much more about what occurs due to the autism, due to the sensory issues, or due to the absolute pitch. The common thread is absolute pitch. Exploring it as a trait segues into understanding the rest of the autism and sensory issues. By peeling those apart, we can then assign the traits to the autism and/or absolute pitch.

The hidden, invisible disability is the most challenging because it goes unrecognized and is often overlooked. What goes on inside your brain is hard for people to identify at one glance. There appear to be no outward markers to identify mental illness, digestive disorders, and sensory issues. People rush to hold the door for the man in the motorized scooter, but nobody in Safeway will dim the lights for your child who's having a meltdown in the freezer aisle. That's okay; we understand—they don't get it because they can't see it. Absolute pitch, however, is something they can see. They can observe this phenomenon in terms they understand and can then grasp that something else is going on. The process of believing what altered perception is and what it can yield begins to unfold.

Many adults have spent years analyzing their own stims and may have developed an awareness that others don't stim. As a result, they've probably learned new stims that they can do privately. When in public, it's common among autistics to chatter the teeth, a simple tap-tap to calm the nerves. Also, pinching/squeezing the toes rhythmically inside their shoes becomes an effective and private defense for expelling "air bubbles" in the lower joints. Finally, small textured fidget toys can be kept in a pocket for a quick rejuvenation. As a young child, Henny learned to "blur" her vision, which she does very often when she can no longer take any more information into her system. As an adult, she learned to remove her glasses or wear tints. To an observer, it appears as if she is staring at nothing, eyes glazed and perhaps inattentive. Inside though, all is calm.

Absolute Pitchers' Stimming

Vocal stims are effective and portable, though not very private. If Henny is walking on a street where there's an overhead train, she might hum a loud monotone in her head so that it vibrates inside, overshadowing the train's sounds. In loud situations, she also finds it helpful to slightly constrict her nasal breathing so she can hear, inside her, the sounds of the air passing through her nose. These soft sounds serve the same purpose as covering her ears.

A client of Susan's related this anecdote about himself: He refused to get onto the San Francisco city bus because it was raining that day, and the bus made a "different sound"—a sound he didn't like, so he waited for the next bus, whose sound was acceptable to him.

For those with absolute pitch, sound engulfs all the senses. Vocal stims provide a multisensory experience, since they're heard auditorily but also felt from within as the voice vibrates internally when produced. A sound that feels comfortable is then latched onto and repeated over and over until a sense of calm is felt. In autism, the production of speech is a mash-up of various areas of skill, and that can cause the brain to hiccup such that the client might be unable to stop on her own. It feels like a car that has flipped upside down but the wheels are still spinning. The client who stims should never be disciplined, asked to stop it, or be ignored. There is value in this coping technique, so grab on to the opportunity.

Musically, vocal stims balance out the pitches of evil. If you have an E coming from the fluorescent light on one side of the room and a B coming from the water pipes on the other side of the room, wouldn't you throw in a G to balance them? Once the vocal stim calms that stimulus, concentration is restored for whatever else is coming at you. Teaching musical concepts helps the individual make sense of the environment and convert that knowledge into a vocabulary that's understood by the world around him.

The art of stimming is to neutralize the sensory stimuli that can lead to overload. If a person can't create these essential tools for himself *on demand*, then he'll be constantly overwhelmed. This leads to furious stimming in an attempt to equalize. Spinning or rocking is a result of extreme overload, in the hope that the movement will create some physical force to shift the internal pressure. Social situations can trigger the brain to be overloaded just as well, and stimming helps alleviate that pain.

Do not force any individual to stop stimming! It's a necessary survival tool. If her stim is inappropriate for public observation, learn to read her signs and develop a new, more appropriate stim that works, or create a situation that eliminates her need to stim. If you were vacationing in a foreign country and didn't speak the language, your vacation would be over the moment you realized that you couldn't even find out how to get to the nearest bathroom. When a person's basic needs are again and again not being met, you can bet she will either become defensive, aggressive, violent, or broken.

Finger twiddling helps one to think. By being conscious of these urges in public, one can twiddle his hands inside his pockets, where he can keep a tiny fidget toy. The "quiet hands" or "sitting on hands" approach to behavior modification is unacceptable. Instead, the environment should be altered so as not to trigger the individual to have to react. Rewarding someone for not flapping is like rewarding him for not wincing when he's in pain.

Self-injurious behavior is a last resort for those trying to get in touch with reality. It's similar to a person pinching herself after a dream to see if she's awake. When her environment has spun out control because the stimuli are constantly overwhelming her, meltdowns happen more and more frequently. These are very traumatic, and the individual might develop post traumatic stress. PTSD (post traumatic stress disorder) develops after a single large traumatic episode, while C-PTSD (complex post traumatic stress disorder) follows an accumulation of repeated small traumas. Grown-up autistics report to have C-PTSD as a result of being forced to minimize their stimming, which leads to constant overload and total meltdowns.

As is true with all survivors of trauma, bringing some element of control back into their lives is the beginning of the healing. For the client who has been pushed over the edge by overload and into a psychiatric state where the benefit of self-injury outweighs the pain, extra care should be taken to respect and understand the reaction to trauma rather than write it off as a standalone mental illness. Trust that the individual's need to check in to see if they are still present is greater than the need to run from pain. This is a last resort response to extreme stimulus such as sensory pain, humiliation (social/emotional), and frustration due to lack of communication. To begin the healing process through music, allow your client to engage in improvisation and to perhaps insert lyrics when you pause during a popular song. Encouraging this level of creation gives birth to an environment where the client feels safe because he or she can control it. Teaching sight-reading empowers such individuals to create sound using a medium of communication not only to interact with others but also quite possibly to control their environment for the first time in their lives.

Musicality

Everyone seems to notice that autistic people possess enormous musicality. Unlocking that appropriately can be a challenge for the untrained, especially with nonverbal children. It's the role of the teacher or music therapist to help the individual demonstrate her strengths so that she can shine.

Using colors to color-code instruments and chords in music is extremely belittling. It's like teaching your nonverbal client to nod yes or no when you ask him or her questions rather than teaching him or her ASL (American Sign Language) or RPM (Rapid Prompting Method). With alternate communication tools, you empower him or her to tell you what he or she wants, independently, rather than waiting for you to ask just the right question as you try to read his mind. If we use traditional music terms with our clients, we can empower them to communicate through music in a language that the rest of the world understands.

The music that you will teach must be at or above age level. If you're concerned about cognition, don't be. People who can't convert thought to speech can still convert thought to letters or gestures. Indeed, a functional-imaging study by Iacoboni et al. (1999) found that Broca's area for speech was activated when people observed and imitated movements, such as sign language[14]. This is evidence that finger movements are able to communicate associations just as speech would, as in the course of the evolution of language when humans first used gestures before spoken language to communicate. If a student can point to a circle or a star on a picture board, he or she can learn that C is here and G is there.

---

[14] Iacoboni, M., Woods, R. P., Brass, M., Bekkering, H., et al. Cortical mechanisms of human imitation. *Science*, 1999, *286*, 2526-2528.

> "Not being able to speak doesn't mean I have nothing to say"
>
> — Unknown

Learning as a Spectrum

People with dyslexia often struggle to decipher words that you spell out for them orally. Henny has long been wondering about developing a method for teaching reading and writing through auditory pitch discrimination. This idea sprang from a sudden realization she had in history class one day. Struggling to process the words on the whiteboard, she focused instead on the sound the ink marker made as the professor wrote the letters out. She became aware that it was so much easier to know what was written if she listened to that sound. Very subtle pitch changes emanate from the rise and fall of the marker pen on the surface of the board, depending on its precise location in relation to the room's acoustics. While this might seem like a sci-fi concept, it could unlock the potential for developing a simple sound-based algorithm for reading comprehension.

Inflexibility is an important need for emotional and academic functioning. You might have a student who appears unmotivated to do anything other than play his or her own songs, which makes you feel like the session is not in your control no matter how hard you try. Put yourself in your student's shoes: he or she has an insatiable need to get this music out—if only he or she can, his or her world falls into place and feels "normal" for those few minutes. This potent ability to connect to the rest of the world should be capitalized upon, not marginalized. Learning music is organizational in nature, which boosts executive function.

It is important that all providers of the service team know what works to stimulate or calm so that one doesn't over-stimulate the child right before the next provider arrives. Learn from each how he or she deals with sensory issues so that all providers carry through a sensory diet in the identical manner. A speech therapist came up with a brilliant strategy for Henny's autistic daughter. Non-speaking and super fidgety, the child struggled to benefit from the 30-minute sessions. When she first arrived for a session, the speech therapist would give her a blank sheet of paper and a hole-puncher to randomly punch holes all over the sheet, then give her a marker and have her draw lines connecting those holes. After that, Henny's daughter was ready to sit still long enough for the session. That simple activity acted as a stim in lieu of squirming, flapping, etc.

Early Intervention

No person in the world has the moral or professional authority to establish a social norm for measuring differences. We continue to demand that people trade their individuality for coexistence in a brutal world. In 1975, Susan completed an internship at a state hospital in Norristown, Pennsylvania. She observed dozens of patients who'd been admitted indefinitely. Many of them would have been diagnosed with autism today. They all sat in the corner, unattended and un-stimulated, day in and day out. The music therapy interns were told not to work with them because these patients had been deemed inappropriate for a group; that is, they would supposedly not benefit from services. Susan and her colleagues heard stories about the workers having no contact with the patients, and even putting their food trays through a slot in the door.

Fast-forward forty years, and we now have a solid EI (early intervention) system established in the United States. EI is critical in the early years of development, as it helps the autistic individual achieve social and sensory milestones through well-researched methodology. While this might not work for all children, it works for many, which makes it a significant resource in the first five years of life.

Carly Fleischman is one example: As a toddler, she got an early diagnosis. Carly lives in Canada, and was given every available intervention. She continued to receive various services, and her parents devoted every waking hour to teaching her, yet Carly presented as profoundly autistic. As a nonverbal teenager, she proved to her family that she could type on a keyboard independently. With a lot of prompting, she bridged the silent world of her mind with the rest of the world, embracing a form of communication understood by most. The TV news episode on Carly is extremely moving, and it proves the point that we don't know what an individual's functioning level is unless she tells us. Carly knew how to read and write, but before she began to communicate through typing, no one knew for sure about her intellect.

Susan knows of a case in which a mom had a Nanny Cam installed to monitor a service provider for her nonverbal son. A review of the recordings showed the woman doing her nails and talking on the phone during the sessions. By being physically present yet allowing the boy to sit there and stim the whole time, she merely kept his oxygen flow intact for survival. Dr. Temple Grandin credits her mother, who in Temple's early childhood years pushed her into a routine for learning. While Temple preferred to stim all day and let the sand flow through her fingers, her mother designed a work/reward regimen that included a stimming timeout schedule for regrouping. Stimming 24/7 eventually gives a person license to retreat into his or her comfort zone for good, making it more difficult for him or her to ever reemerge.

The means to demonstrate intelligence is the parent's responsibility. If a person supposedly can't read or write, then how will she prove her intelligence? Standardized testing is designed to exploit weaknesses. Educators and clinicians will work only to the goals the parents set, yet parents who've lost expectations assume that because professional testing results were low, they were indicative of low functioning. Educability is then sadly underestimated.

Coda: In the Key of Henny

In the summer of 2012, I observed a special education classroom in the Oakland school district of California's East Bay area. This poor neighborhood benefitted from several excellent teachers, who received tuition waivers in college if they contracted with the state to teach in inner-city schools. On that particular day, I observed Mr. Nolan Hutton's classroom and was very impressed with his desire to learn from my observations. He encouraged me to to interrupt his lessons if there was any technique that could be implemented immediately in real time.

Before the students were given their math worksheets, they were instructed to finish them quietly, and then form a line at the teacher's desk for grading. It is important to note that all the students had an IEP (Individualized Education Plan), and a vast mishmash of special needs. Many of them fidgeted and couldn't remain focused on any direction for more than a minute or two, and breaks were frequent. When the students got up to form the line, it became clear to me that some ideas were needed for them to be able to remain still long enough for a line to be distinguishable. As I watched the little bobbleheads fidgeting, jumping, flapping, stimming, and mumbling, I could see that their physical movement was a result of their efforts to be still.

I approached Mr. Hutton and whispered something into his ear. He responded with a "humor me" face, and decided to try my latest whacky suggestion. Following my direction, Mr. Hutton told the students to stand in line, and make "piano toes". He explained, "Squeeze your toes inside your shoes, and play a little song while you stay in line". As if a magic spell was cast over the room, the little angels formed a line with military-precision, and their precious faces reflected the intense concentration they exerted as they tried to audiate the songs in their heads, as played by their little piggies. To this day, piano toes help me stay calm in the world around me. I use them as a private coping technique that has carried me from infancy into adulthood.

I was that kid who played songs on the keypad of the cordless telephone. I was also that kid who ran to my toy xylophone to recreate the siren of the fire truck that had just passed the house. I had no idea back then that these were all characteristics of an individual with absolute pitch. As a child, my gifts were expressed in a way that got me into quite a few awkward situations. I always knew who was being called on the phone based on the tones of the phone number.

Sometimes, the recognition would trigger grand announcements of private information such as, "You just called aunt Leah" or "your pincode is 4-1-6-7". While I thought this was so obvious and cool, others thought it was uncalled for and inappropriate.

As an undiagnosed autistic in a strict religious and insular community, my strengths and unique abilities were targeted rather than treasured. In a world that values conformity above all, I stood out and was systematically silenced. My natural ways of functioning were classified as opposition and defiance and I was thus disciplined for what authorities perceived as inappropriate and immoral behaviour. "Why can't you just do it normally like everyone else?" were the words that dominated every interaction I had with others.

Autistic people with absolute pitch are masters at imitating voices, sounds, and accents from movies and other mediums. Denied access to those sources as a child, my religious version of those behaviors was quite similar. Instead of repeating movie scenes, I used to spout lines from psalms and other prayers. I would throw them into conversation where I saw fit, which left people around me scratching their heads, trying to understand the out-of-context references. Now I know this as autistic scripting behavior. These uncanny abilities prevail in similar forms regardless of culture and geography.

After returning home from the synagogue, I'd spend an enormous amount of time imitating the cantors and rabbis. I was intrigued with memorizing and perfecting the intricate chapter readings of sacred text chanted in the ancient trope tradition. I loved struggling to get simple melodies out of the *shofar*, even though it was known to produce only one wailing pitch for Rosh Hashanah. These traditions were not a girl's place to recreate, and I was shamed for my interests in "boys stuff." Singing or making music on instruments was prohibited for girls for modesty reasons.

My autism was undiagnosed until I was thirty-two. By that time I was already on my second life journey. Seeing all the parallels between my children's development and my memories of my own childhood led me to seek out my own diagnosis. Personally, it was life altering, in a good way. I did not see myself as a disabled person and still don't. The diagnosis gave me permission to mourn the loss of time and energy spent on fitting in and making myself pass for normal. I no longer had to commit to spending the rest of my life working on myself and refining my character, without accessing my strengths.

For my thirty-fifth birthday I got a present from my friend Arla. It was a bracelet with the inscription DREAMS BECOME REALITY ONE CHOICE AT A TIME. How appropriate at just the time when I was fighting so hard to explore my individual strengths for myself by getting an education under increasingly difficult circumstances. My quest for education came with harsh consequences doled out by my community of origin, and I had to choose between my old life and my unknown future.

I didn't know how much of a door had opened to me when my children were diagnosed. Despite my background without access to secular and classical music or orchestral music of any kind, I passed auditions on piano at six colleges across the country after memorizing three classical pieces from YouTube the night before. In my first music theory class, I found out that the keys on the piano had names. Three weeks later, I learned enough of the fundamentals to compose my first piece, a piano trio.

While I was an undergraduate, I struggled with the consequences of being a non-traditional student: I was the only parent in the entire college student body and everyone was half my age. Moreover, my own unique neurology led me to question the philosophies of the discipline which led to intense clashes with the department. The institution where I was studying music therapy was heavily focused on canonical theory and unwelcoming to questions regarding the philosophies of the discipline. These clashes with the department forced me to make some hard decisions at the end of my undergraduate studies.

At this stage of my life, I was no longer willing to be controlled by people who felt threatened by my nonconformity. Unabashedly continuing to question the status quo shaped my current work and spurred the scientific curiosity which has lead to my scholarly endeavors to date. Learning to read musical notation in my late 30's was the key to unlocking my individuality. Composing music is my happy place, as I have complete control in creating sound that others must follow when playing the score. I now know that being told how to do my work and be squeezed into the box of someone else's imagination will bring me dangerously close to duplicating their life's mistakes.

When I observe autistic individuals, I can feel the pain and emotions inside them. Their stims and behaviors and words are so clear to me, as we're perfectly in sync. The power of this ability is best put to use when I observe an entire classroom and within twenty minutes, can summarize my recommendations for the educational team. My work as a consultant grew into a career of entering diverse environments and performing sensory audits. I can tell a school that a specific light makes a noise, and that a minor modification could be made with tremendous results. I earned my nickname, the *Autism Whisperer* in the summer of 2013 in California.

When the teachers get excited and begin asking questions, the real work begins. They usually ask something like "So tell me, when this kid does this thing, what does it mean?" Small suggestions make a huge difference immediately. My most exciting observation was when I advised the teacher to remove "can you?" from each direction he gave to the class. I suggested he avoid "When you're done with your math, can you please put your papers in your folder, and can you please put your folder inside your desk?" Autistic individuals who may think in a literal manner will silently respond to a "can you?" with a "yes." Students think that what the person is looking for is an affirmation that they can perform the activity, rather than directing them to do it. The miscommunication often results in students in being disciplined for not following directions. Situations like this are easily remedied when the root of the word *directions* (direct!) is applied.

Currently, I teach nonverbal, autistic, and special-needs students to sight-read music for piano in the classical tradition. I teach all my students via Skype/FaceTime to reach those in underserved areas. Skype eliminates the need for travel, transition, and sensory accommodation. The student also knows that when she's had enough, she can "hit the panic button" and end the call. With strategic placement of the screens, I can be in the student's environment without being in her face.

Using Skype as a conduit for maintaining a global practice, I incorporate musical paraphrasing to validate client expression. The reciprocity of sound teaches the client that he has been heard and understood. As someone with absolute pitch, I'm finely tuned to the vast spectrum of ways in which AP manifests itself. In recognizing such abilities, I promote a fluid learning environment based on the strengths that AP adds to the learning process. When I teach to the gift, the strengths eventually overshadow the weaknesses that were previously pathologized. Musical empowerment is the first step needed for nonverbal people to be valued in a speaking world as abled beings.

This poem is dedicated to all those who are still struggling to be heard:

Words

Words. They are stuck.
It's stuck in my throat.
No place to go.

Easing it out with very little tools
Sharp objects obstructing its path
Worrying its way through. There.

Some words still left behind
Deeper down in the pit
In the stomach, hastening to escape.

Unsure how to let go
How to form itself into a phrase
Is it too sharp, is it too loose?

Will it hurt others
As much as it hurts me?
Should I bury it for eternity?

It tumbles around and spins inside
The ruckus is overpowering
Jumbled. Bumping into the walls.

Loud noises of chaos from within
Unable to stifle, patience wearing thin.
How to transition from this phase?

What will these thoughts reflect
To those who land with it
And what will they perceive it to be?

Once it is out, it is free
Free of me but free for them too
And never can you know, what they will do.

For 'tis the soul
That weaves your essence into cloth
Sparkling in the sun with its glint.

Taking with you a story of your past
To wear on your sleeves for all to see
True intentions, merely a hint.

Inhibitions exploding like a raging sea
Cloudless skies not marring your thoughts
Your words are free to soar.

Made in the USA
Coppell, TX
26 August 2020